Easy Cooking
THE COSTCO WAY™

Hass Avocado and Blueberry Fruit Salad can be found on page 41.

Easy Cooking
THE COSTCO WAY™

Favorite recipes using Costco products

Tim Talevich
Editorial Director

With a foreword by
Kathy Casey

Issaquah, Washington

Publisher:	David W. Fuller
Editorial Director:	Tim Talevich
Art Director:	Doris Winters
Associate Editor:	Judy Gouldthorpe
Contributing Editor:	Pat Volchok
Graphic Designers:	Dawna Tessier
	Brenda Tradii
Photographers:	Darren Emmens
	Tom Clements
	Chris McArthur
	Norman Hersom
	Devin Seferos
Food Stylists:	Amy Muzyka-McGuire
	Jane Morimoto
	Chris Jackson
	Joanne Naganawa
Kitchen Manager:	Linda Carey
Studio Assistant:	Rozarri Lynch
Business Manager:	Jane Klein-Shucklin
Advertising Manager:	Steve Trump
Advertising Assistant:	Aliw Moral
Production Manager:	Pam Sather
Assistant Production Manager:	Antolin Matsuda
Color Specialist:	MaryAnne Robbers
Proofreader:	Shana McNally
Distribution:	Rossie Cruz

All photographs by Iridio Photography,
with the following exceptions:
© 2003 E. Jane Armstrong, 7
Heinz, 81 (top left)
Heinz, 101 (top right)
Chicken of the Sea, 126 (top left)
Sunkist, 140 (top left)
Nonni's, 156 (top left)
Masterfood, 168 (top right)
Kozyshack, 173 (top right)
Starbuck's, 187

FIRST EDITION

Photography by Iridio Photography, Seattle
Printed and bound in the United States of America
by Quebecor World at Kingsport Press

ISBN 0-9722164-3-X
Library of Congress Control Number: 2004113770

118

91

182

174

37

43

13

68

Contents

To Our Valued Members ▌

We are delighted to offer you our new book, *Easy Cooking the Costco Way*, as a token of our appreciation for your loyal membership in Costco Wholesale.

As you might expect from Costco, *Easy Cooking the Costco Way* has a heavy emphasis on quality and value—whether it is what you buy or what you serve. Just as in our warehouses, the emphasis here is on the basics—meat, potatoes and some great salmon.

But, just as in our warehouses, there is always an unexpected treasure to be discovered—like our special section on page 88 with recipes from member Rhonda Barranco that feature our famous Costco rotisserie chicken in a variety of dishes, our special collection of salmon recipes from members on page 128 or our quick-fix smoothies recipes beginning on page 181.

We've also included recipes for appetizers, beverages, desserts and more, with the common themes being easy preparation and a great result.

This book has been made possible through the support of Costco's many suppliers. These are the same vendors who work so closely with our Costco buyers to constantly improve the quality and value of the food products we sell. At our request, they have come up with some great ways to prepare their specialties, all with an emphasis on simplicity and ease in the kitchen.

Costco has a long tradition as an innovator in food retailing, and we hope you will enjoy these recipes using some of our favorite products.

Bon appétite!

Ginnie Roeglin,
Senior Vice President,
E-commerce and Publishing

Wow! Costco's third cookbook! With more than 250 recipes from 200 suppliers, *Easy Cooking the Costco Way* features Costco products, so you can easily find the ingredients you need at a great price. And since the theme is "easy cooking," this book is sure to get a lot of use. The recipes cover the gastronomic gamut from quickly assembled, everyday meals to dinner-party appetizers—and even breakfast. You *will* be inspired to cook.

Everyone is crunched for time these days, so easy recipes have big appeal. While there's nothing better than cooking up some homemade goodness from scratch, more often than not there just aren't enough hours in the day to make everything yourself. But with Costco's huge variety of products, you can pull together a quickie meal or go all out and spend the day cooking.

Being able to purchase great products makes cooking meals easy and delicious. The wonderful practicality of prewashed spinach or mesclun, for example, is a cook's blessing. Then there are already-cleaned mushrooms, stir-fry veggies, and fresh orange and grapefruit sections. Many recipes in this volume take advantage of the ready-to-use produce available at various times of the year at Costco.

And with so many cool prepared sauces, salsas and toppings available, looking like a gourmet chef is easy. Then there's the Costco rotisserie chicken—a busy-schedule dinner essential! There are so many ways to use it, and *Easy Cooking the Costco Way* illustrates a few of them well.

Almost everyone I know has bought the five-pound bags of meatballs in the freezer section. Pop them in a baker, douse them with tomato herb sauce, dollop on a little pesto and feta cheese, then bake them up. Voila! Serve them with Italian-style focaccia warm from the oven—reheated, of course!

You'll also find great recipes for spreads, breads, cheeses and more. It's super simple to wrap a luscious Brie in a pastry crust—made with refrigerated crescent rolls—and then bake till warm and oozy.

And scope out some yummy sweet endings. *Easy Cooking the Costco Way* features some fun ideas using premade cheesecake and brownies. Frozen cream puffs topped with fudge and/or caramel sauce are the perfect luscious nibble.

This is an excellent opportunity to try new products, and these easy recipes from Costco suppliers show you what to do with them. *Easy Cooking the Costco Way* will introduce you to new flavors and new ways to cook when your time is at a premium. And you'll have more time to sit back, relax and enjoy.

Costco member and chef Kathy Casey is a food, beverage and restaurant-concept consultant and food writer. She owns Kathy Casey Food Studios and Dish D'Lish. See more at her Web site, www.kathycasey.com.

Kathy Casey

About This Book ▍

S ince publishing our first Costco cookbook two years ago, we have had many positive comments from members who have enjoyed the recipes and tips in *Entertaining the Costco Way* and *Cooking the Costco Way*. We are excited this year to be able to offer a third cookbook that is just as full of fantastic ways to prepare the wide range of food we sell. In fact, we are so excited about this book that we are offering it as a gift to those members who visit our warehouses the weekend after Thanksgiving (as long as the supply lasts!) Unlike the previous two books, *Easy Cooking the Costco Way* will not be sold in our warehouses or on costco.com.

As the name implies, *Easy Cooking the Costco Way* emphasizes recipes that take a minimal amount of preparation time. It can be used as a companion to the two earlier books, fitting nicely on the kitchen bookshelf as part of a set, or it will work just as well as a stand-alone. It is as easy to use as its recipes are to prepare, with sections on breakfast, appetizers, salads and soups, side dishes, entrées, desserts and beverages.

As before, our vendors have supplied recipes that show off their products in the most tantalizing ways. Please note that each recipe has been identified with the vendor's corporate name and logo. Some branded products may not be sold in your part of the country. In such cases, you should substitute a similar product.

I hope you enjoy this token of our appreciation for your membership in Costco and that you derive many hours of dining pleasure from *Easy Cooking the Costco Way*.

David W. Fuller
Publisher

Easy Cooking
THE COSTCO WAY™

Breakfast

KELLOGG'S EGGO
Western Waffles ◄

12 Kellogg's Eggo Homestyle Waffles, toasted
2 cups shredded low-fat Swiss cheese
1 cup diced smoked turkey breast
1 cup low-fat sour cream
1 cup egg substitute
1/2 teaspoon salt
1/2 teaspoon garlic powder
1/2 teaspoon black pepper

1. Preheat oven to 350°F.
2. Place waffles on a foil-lined 18-by-26-by-1-inch sheet pan coated with cooking spray. Evenly top each waffle with cheese and turkey.
3. Combine sour cream, egg substitute, salt, garlic powder and pepper in a bowl and spread evenly over the waffles.
4. Bake for 25 minutes, or until set and lightly browned. Serve hot. Makes 12 servings.

MICHAEL FOODS
Asparagus and Parmesan Frittata ▲

12 ounces trimmed asparagus
2 tablespoons olive oil
1 garlic clove, minced
Salt and black pepper
16 ounces Kirkland Signature™ Egg Starts
1/2 cup grated Parmigiano-Reggiano cheese
1 tablespoon fresh thyme leaves
Parmigiano-Reggiano shavings
Fresh thyme sprigs

1. Cut asparagus stems into 1/4-inch slices; leave tips whole.
2. Heat oil in a large skillet over medium heat. Add asparagus; cook for 3 minutes, or until crisp-tender. Add garlic and cook for 30 seconds. Season to taste with salt and pepper.
3. In a bowl, combine Egg Starts and grated cheese; add to the skillet. Reduce heat and cook until eggs are set on the bottom and around the edges. Sprinkle thyme leaves over eggs. Lift the sides, allowing the mixture to flow under the edges until no longer runny. Sprinkle with cheese shavings to taste.
4. Cover and cook over low heat for 10 minutes, or until set. Loosen edges, slide onto a serving plate and garnish with thyme sprigs. Serve warm or at room temperature. Makes 4 servings.

Breakfast ▮

HORMEL
Scrambled Bacon Burritos

1 tablespoon oil
1 cup sliced green bell pepper
1 cup sliced fresh mushrooms
1/2 cup sliced red onion
1 teaspoon minced garlic
6 eggs, beaten
6 8-inch flour tortillas
1 1/2 cups shredded Colby and Monterey Jack cheese
3 1/2 ounces (1/2 cup) Hormel* Premium Crumbled Bacon or Kirkland Signature/Hormel fully cooked bacon, crumbled
Chi-Chi's* salsa
Sour cream

1. Preheat oven to 350°F.
2. Heat oil in a large skillet over medium heat. Add bell pepper, mushrooms, onion and garlic and cook until tender; remove from pan.
3. Add eggs to pan and cook until lightly scrambled. Stir in vegetables.
4. Spoon eggs down center of each tortilla. Sprinkle with cheese and bacon. Roll up tortillas and place seam side down in a 9-by-13-inch pan. Bake for 5-8 minutes, or until heated through. Serve with salsa and sour cream. Makes 6 servings.

Brands may vary by region; substitute a similar product.

LAND O' LAKES
Cottage Cheese Muffins

1/4 cup granulated sugar
1 3/4 teaspoons ground cinnamon, divided
1 cup Land O Lakes* Cottage Cheese
1/2 cup firmly packed brown sugar
1/3 cup Land O Lakes* Fresh Buttery Taste Spread
2 eggs
1 1/2 cups all-purpose flour
1 teaspoon baking soda
1/2 cup raisins

1. Preheat oven to 375°F.
2. Combine granulated sugar and 1/2 teaspoon cinnamon in a small bowl. Set aside.
3. Combine cottage cheese, brown sugar, Fresh Buttery Taste Spread and eggs in a large bowl. Beat at medium speed until creamy. Add flour, 1 1/4 teaspoons cinnamon and baking soda; stir just until moistened. Stir in raisins.
4. Spoon batter into 12 paper-lined muffin pan cups. Sprinkle each with 1 teaspoon of the topping. Bake for 20-25 minutes, or until lightly browned. Serve warm muffins with Fresh Buttery Taste Spread. Makes 12 muffins.

Brands may vary by region; substitute a similar product.

Where simple goodness begins.™

SUNSET
Summer Quiche by Mastronardi Produce ▼

1 bunch of asparagus
1 loaf day-old French bread, cut in 1-inch slices
1 small onion, finely chopped
1/4 each Sunset red and yellow bell peppers, finely chopped
2 tablespoons chopped fresh basil
1/2 cup shredded Colby cheese
1/2 cup shredded Monterey Jack cheese
1/2 cup shredded Cheddar cheese
8 large eggs
2 cups skim milk
1/2 teaspoon salt
1/2 teaspoon black pepper
1 teaspoon Dijon mustard
10 Sunset Campari tomatoes, sliced

1. Preheat oven to 350°F.
2. Cut asparagus into bite-size pieces and blanch in boiling water until tender. Drain, chill in cold water and drain.
3. Place bread slices in a greased 9-by-13-inch baking dish. Spread asparagus, onion, peppers, basil and cheese evenly over the bread.
4. In a bowl, whisk together eggs, milk, salt, pepper and mustard; pour over the vegetables. Arrange tomatoes evenly on top, covering the entire area.
5. Bake for 70 minutes, or until lightly browned. This dish can be refrigerated overnight and baked in the morning. Makes 10 servings.

Breakfast ▌

TARANTINO'S
Breakfast Turnovers ▼

1 pound Tarantino's* breakfast sausage links, casings removed
1 small red onion, julienned
1 medium apple, peeled and diced
1 ½ cups halved red seedless grapes
1 pound puff pastry (2 sheets)
8 ounces Cheddar cheese, shredded
1 egg, beaten

1. Preheat oven to 375°F.
2. In a large sauté pan over medium heat, sauté sausage, breaking up the meat to brown evenly. Remove from the pan to a large bowl.
3. In the same pan, sauté onions until softened. Add apples and sauté for 2 minutes. Add grapes and heat through. Combine sautéed onions and fruit with the sausage. Set aside to cool.

4. On a lightly floured work surface, roll out each sheet of pastry to measure 14 by 14 inches. Cut each sheet of pastry into 4 equal squares. Divide the filling and shredded cheese evenly among the 8 pastry squares. Fold in half to form a triangle and crimp the edges with a fork. Brush with beaten egg.
5. Bake the turnovers on a parchment-lined baking sheet for 20 minutes, or until golden brown. Serve warm. Makes 8 servings.

Recipe provided by Chef Katherine Emmenegger, CCC.
Brands may vary by region; substitute a similar product.

GEORGE WESTON BAKERIES
Shrimp Louis Muffins

1 cup mayonnaise

1/2 cup chili sauce

1 tablespoon minced parsley

1 teaspoon lemon juice

1 teaspoon horseradish

1/4 cup finely chopped onion

1/8 teaspoon salt

1/8 teaspoon pepper

4 Thomas' Original Flavor English Muffins, split, toasted and buttered

Lettuce leaves

4 hard-boiled eggs, sliced

3/4 pound medium shrimp, shelled, deveined and cooked

1. In a small bowl, combine mayonnaise, chili sauce, parsley, lemon juice, horseradish, onion, salt and pepper; stir until blended. Cover and chill.

2. Top each muffin half with lettuce, egg slices, shrimp and dressing. Makes 4 servings.

George Weston Bakeries Inc.

KRUSTEAZ
Crêpes

1/2 cup Krusteaz Buttermilk Pancake Mix

1/2 cup all-purpose flour

1 cup water

2 eggs, beaten

1 tablespoon butter, melted

1 tablespoon sugar

1. In a small bowl, stir together pancake mix and flour; add water gradually. Add eggs and stir to blend. Stir butter and sugar together and mix into the batter. Let stand for 20-30 minutes.

2. Preheat a lightly greased 5- to 6-inch frying pan or crêpe pan over medium-high heat. Spoon about 1 tablespoon batter in the center of the pan, tilting to coat the pan evenly. Just a thin layer of batter should cover the pan. Cook until delicately browned; turn and cook lightly on the other side. Makes 18-24 crêpes.

For breakfast: Fill crêpes with fresh or frozen (thawed and drained) berries. Roll up and sprinkle with confectioners' sugar.

For brunch: Fill crêpes with chopped cooked spinach and ricotta cheese. Roll up and top with marinara sauce, if desired. Sprinkle with grated mozzarella cheese and place under broiler until bubbling hot.

KRUSTEAZ

KIRKLAND SIGNATURE/MULTIFOODS
Blueberry Muffin French Toast ▼

2 eggs, beaten
1/3 cup milk
3 fresh Kirkland Signature blueberry muffins, cut in 4 equal slices
1 cup confectioners' sugar
4 large fresh strawberries, hulled and sliced
1 11-ounce can mandarin oranges
1 1/2 cups fresh or frozen blueberries
1 cup blueberry-flavored syrup

1. Combine eggs and milk. Dip each muffin slice in egg mixture. Heat a skillet coated with nonstick cooking spray over medium-high heat; cook muffin slices until golden brown on each side.

2. Arrange 3 slices on each plate and sprinkle with confectioners' sugar. Serve with fruit and syrup. Makes 4 servings.

PROFOOD
Spicy Mango Breakfast Jam ▼

2 cups chopped Philippine Brand dried mangoes

3 cups Philippine Brand mango juice

1/2 cup chopped mild onion

2 tablespoons chopped cilantro

1-2 tablespoons seeded, minced serrano or other small chile, optional

1 teaspoon grated lime peel

2 teaspoons lime juice

1/4 teaspoon ground cumin

Peasant bread, thickly sliced and toasted

1. Place dried mangoes in a bowl. Heat mango juice to a boil and pour over the dried mangoes. Let soak until tender and most of the liquid is absorbed (1 hour or longer). Strain, retaining leftover juices.

2. Quickly blend mangoes, onion, cilantro, chile, lime peel, lime juice and cumin in a food processor to make a spicy jam. Drizzle reserved mango juice on the toasted bread and top with jam. Makes about 3 cups.

ProFood

DELANO FARMS
Breakfast Compote ◄

2 cups halved assorted Delano Farms* grapes
   (Crimson, Princess, Globes and Flames)

2 cups sliced strawberries

1 cup cubed melon

3 peaches or nectarines, cubed

1 pint blueberries

3 tablespoons honey

$1/4$ cup fresh orange juice

1 teaspoon cinnamon

2-3 tablespoons sour cream

1. Place fruit in a large bowl and toss gently.

2. Whisk together honey, orange juice and cinnamon in a small bowl; stir into the fruit mixture. Refrigerate for 30 minutes.

3. Serve with a dollop of sour cream. Makes 6-8 servings.

Brands may vary by region; substitute a similar product.

KIRSCHENMAN
Chocolate-Dipped Brunch Grapes ▲

8 ounces dark chocolate

8 ounces white chocolate

4 pounds Kirschenman individual large seedless grapes or
   smaller seedless grape bunches

1. Line cookie sheets with either waxed paper or parchment paper.

2. Melt dark chocolate over simmering water in a double boiler. Stir until chocolate is melted and smooth. Do not overheat. Repeat with white chocolate.

3. Reserve half of the grapes (2 pounds). Dry the remaining grapes thoroughly. Immerse larger grapes entirely in either dark or white chocolate. Remove with a fork and place on a lined cookie sheet. If using grape bunches, dip bottom of bunches in either dark or white chocolate. (If using green, black and red grapes, dip green grapes in dark chocolate and black and red grapes in white chocolate.)

4. Let all dipped fruit set up in the refrigerator until chocolate is no longer soft to the touch and fruit peels off the lined cookie sheet easily.

5. To serve, arrange the chocolate-coated grapes with the reserved grapes. Dipped fruit, refrigerated, will keep for 2 days. Do not freeze. Makes 12 servings.

Breakfast

SAMSONS
Fruit Breakfast Teacups ▲

1/4 cup sugar

2 teaspoons cornstarch

1/2 cup orange juice

2 tablespoons butter

2 each: Fowler Packing nectarines, peaches, plums and apricots, sliced

1/2 pound red seedless grapes, halved

3 tablespoons apricot preserves

8 teacups

1. Combine sugar and cornstarch in a small saucepan. Stir in orange juice. Cook over medium heat, stirring frequently, until it comes to a full boil. Boil for 2 minutes; remove from heat and stir in butter. Cool.

2. Meanwhile, toss fruit together in a bowl and then place in teacups.

3. Drizzle orange sauce over the fruit and add a dollop of apricot preserves. Makes 8 servings.

FOUR STAR FRUIT
Breakfast Drink ▲

1/2 cup Four Star seedless grapes

1/2 banana

1/4 cup milk

1/2 cup plain yogurt

1-2 tablespoons honey

1/4 teaspoon fresh lemon juice

2-3 ice cubes

Combine grapes, banana, milk, yogurt, honey, lemon juice and ice in a blender. Process on high speed for 15 seconds. Serve immediately. Makes 1 serving.

ALPINE FRESH
Mango-Banana Fruit Drink

2 ripe Alpine Fresh* mangoes, peeled, pitted and coarsely chopped
1 ripe banana, peeled
1 cup low-fat yogurt
4-6 ice cubes
Sprigs of fresh mint

1. Combine mangoes, banana, yogurt and ice in a blender. Process until smooth. Pour into glasses and garnish with a mint sprig. (Strain first if desired.)
2. Add a little milk if the drink is too thick. Add 1-2 tablespoons brown sugar for more sweetness. Makes 4 servings.

Brands may vary by region; substitute a similar product.

KIRKLAND SIGNATURE/SILK
Straw-Nana Smoothie

1 cup Kirkland Signature/Silk Vanilla Soymilk
1/2 cup diced frozen strawberries
1 frozen banana, sliced
2 tablespoons sweetener of choice (optional)
1/8 teaspoon vanilla extract (optional)

In a blender, combine Silk Vanilla Soymilk, strawberries, banana, sweetener and vanilla. Blend until smooth and creamy. Makes 2 servings.

Silk

Appetizers

EINSTEIN BROS. BAGELS
Grilled Bagel and Three-Pepper Bruschetta ◀

1 each yellow, red and green bell pepper
2 cups vine-ripe tomatoes cut in 1/2-inch cubes
2 tablespoons extra-virgin olive oil
2 teaspoons minced fresh garlic
1 teaspoon balsamic vinegar
1/4 cup chopped fresh basil
Salt and pepper
4 Kirkland Signature by Noah's New York* plain bagels
Olive oil
Asiago cheese

1. Preheat grill.
2. Grill, peel and dice peppers in 1/2-inch cubes. Combine peppers, tomatoes, extra-virgin olive oil, garlic, vinegar, basil, and salt and pepper to taste in a mixing bowl.
3. Split bagels in half. Lightly brush oil on cut side of bagels. Grill to desired crispness.
4. Slice the grilled bagel halves in half again so that you have 4 grilled pieces per bagel. Spread evenly with the topping. Garnish with shaved Asiago cheese and serve on a platter. Makes 12-16 servings.

Brands may vary by region; substitute a similar product.

BC HOT HOUSE
Tricolor Tomato Bruschetta ▲

2 1/2 cups chopped seeded BC Hot House* tricolor
 (red, yellow, orange) tomatoes
8-10 sun-dried tomatoes, chopped
1/2 cup chopped green onion
1/2 cup chopped fresh basil
2 garlic cloves, minced
1 tablespoon balsamic vinegar
2 tablespoons olive oil
1 cup grated Parmesan cheese
Salt and pepper
1 baguette loaf
Olive oil cooking spray

1. Place tomatoes in a sieve and let drain. In a bowl, combine tomatoes, sun-dried tomatoes, green onion, basil, garlic, vinegar, oil, Parmesan, and salt and pepper to taste. Let stand at room temperature for several hours.
2. Preheat broiler. Cut 16 half-inch slices from the baguette and place on a baking sheet. Spray both sides of slices with olive oil spray. Toast on both sides under the broiler.
3. To serve, top each slice of baguette toast with a heaping mound of topping. Makes 4-6 servings.

Brands may vary by region; substitute a similar product.

KIRKLAND SIGNATURE
Flatbread Mozzarella Bruschetta ▲

6 tablespoons chopped roasted red peppers
1/4 cup chopped black olives
1 loaf Kirkland Signature Garlic Butter Flatbread
2 cups fresh mozzarella broken in small pieces

1. Preheat oven to 375°F.
2. Spread red peppers and olives evenly over each half of bread. Spread evenly with mozzarella.
3. Place on a baking sheet and bake for 20 minutes, or until lightly browned. Remove from the oven and let cool for 5 minutes on a wire rack. Slice each half into 10 pieces and serve immediately. Makes 10 servings.
Pesto Bruschetta variation: Bake bread butter side up for 10 minutes. Remove from the oven and spread with 2/3 cup prepared pesto. Top with 6 tablespoons chopped sun-dried tomatoes and 1/4 cup chopped black olives. Bake 10 minutes longer.

HIDDEN VALLEY THE ORIGINAL RANCH
Provolone Melt ▲

1 piece focaccia bread (approx. 10 by 7 by 3/4 inches)
2 cups shredded rotisserie chicken (option: ham or cooked turkey)
1/2 cup Hidden Valley The Original Ranch Dressing
1/4 cup diagonally sliced green onions
2 medium tomatoes, thinly sliced
4 ounces provolone cheese, sliced (option: Cheddar or Swiss cheese)
2 tablespoons grated Parmesan cheese

1. Preheat broiler. Place focaccia on a baking sheet.
2. Stir together chicken, dressing and green onions in a bowl. Arrange mixture evenly on top of focaccia.
3. Add a layer of sliced tomatoes and a layer of provolone cheese. Sprinkle with Parmesan.
4. Broil for 2 minutes, or until cheese is melted and bubbly. Makes 4 servings.

SANTA SWEETS
Italian Bruschetta ▼

1 pint Santa Sweets* grape tomatoes, halved

2 celery ribs, diced

1/4 cup pitted black olives, sliced

1/3 cup stuffed green olives, sliced

1/4 cup minced parsley

1 small garlic clove, minced

1 large carrot, julienned

1/3 sweet onion, finely minced

1 tablespoon virgin olive oil

1/2 tablespoon balsamic vinegar

Salt and freshly ground pepper to taste

12 slices Italian or French bread, 3/4 inch thick

1. Combine tomatoes, celery, olives, parsley, garlic, carrot, onion, oil, vinegar, and salt and pepper in a large bowl. Taste and correct seasoning if needed. Let stand at room temperature for about 30 minutes.

2. Grill or broil bread slices. Spoon topping onto toast. Makes 6 servings.

*Brands may vary by region; substitute a similar product.

Appetizers █

WINDSET FARMS
Spicy Tomato Bruschetta ▼

1 baguette

6 tablespoons extra-virgin
   olive oil, divided

12 Windset Farms* tomatoes-on-
   the-vine, 6 red and 6 yellow,
   seeded and finely diced

4 garlic cloves, finely minced

2 small jalapeño peppers,
   seeded and minced

1/2 cup chopped fresh basil

Generous pinches of salt and
   freshly ground black pepper

6 ounces soft, mild goat cheese

1. Preheat oven to 325°F. Cut baguette diagonally into 24 slices; arrange on a baking sheet. Brush both sides of bread slices with 2 tablespoons of the olive oil. Bake until toasted and golden, about 6 minutes per side.

2. Combine 4 tablespoons olive oil, tomatoes, garlic, jalapeños, basil, and salt and pepper to taste in a medium bowl.

3. Spread goat cheese over toast; arrange in a single layer on a baking sheet. Mound tomato mixture on toast. Bake on the center oven rack until heated through, 5-8 minutes. Transfer bruschetta to a platter and serve immediately. Makes 12 servings.

Tip: Toast and tomatoes can be prepared 1 hour ahead. Cover and store separately at room temperature.

* Brands may vary by region; substitute a similar product.

windset
FARMS

DARE FOODS
Stuffed Gouda Cheese ▲

1 14-ounce (approx.) whole Gouda cheese in wax
1 teaspoon prepared yellow mustard
2 1/2 teaspoons red wine (or Worcestershire sauce)
1 tablespoon chopped fresh tarragon,
   or 1 teaspoon dried tarragon, crushed
Green onion, sliced
Breton, Cabaret or other Dare* crackers

1. Slice approximately 1 inch off the top of the cheese, cutting right through the plastic wrap and wax. Using a sharp paring knife or melon baller, hollow out the cheese, leaving a 1/2-inch shell. Remove the plastic wrap but not the wax.

2. Shred the scooped-out cheese on the smallest shredder blade of a food processor. Place shredded cheese, mustard, wine and tarragon in a large bowl and toss lightly with a fork. Spoon the mixture into the Gouda shell. There should be enough to fill the shell twice.

3. Sprinkle with green onions. Serve with a selection of Dare crackers. Makes 12-15 servings.

Brands may vary by region; substitute a similar product.

MAKING EVERY DAY DELICIOUS.

EMERIL'S
Con Queso ▲

2 tablespoons vegetable oil
1 cup chopped yellow onion
1 teaspoon Emeril's Original Essence*
1 cup chopped seeded tomato
1 teaspoon minced garlic
8 ounces white Cheddar cheese, shredded
8 ounces Monterey Jack cheese, shredded
1 cup chopped canned mild green chiles
3 tablespoons sour cream
1 teaspoon ground white pepper
1/4 teaspoon salt
Tortilla chips

1. Heat vegetable oil in a medium saucepan over medium heat until hot, about 1 minute.

2. Add onion and Emeril's Original Essence and cook, stirring, until soft, about 5 minutes.

3. Stir in tomato and garlic and cook, stirring, for another 2 minutes.

4. Reduce heat to medium-low and add cheeses and chiles. Cook, stirring constantly, until cheese melts, about 2 minutes.

5. Stir in sour cream, white pepper and salt. Serve immediately with tortilla chips. Makes 6-8 servings.

Brands may vary by region; substitute a similar product.

Appetizers I

HEINZ
Big Game Party Platter ▼

Poppers* Cream Cheese Jalapeños
Delimex* Beef and Cheese Taquitos
Ore-Ida* Bagel Bites Deluxe Pepperoni & Cheese

1. Preheat oven to 450°F. Place 7 poppers on an unlined, ungreased cookie sheet, spaced well apart. Bake for 7 minutes on the middle rack.
2. Remove from the oven and add 7 Taquitos and 7 Bagel Bites. Bake 7 minutes longer.
3. Remove from the oven and let sit 1 minute before serving. Makes 4 servings.

* Brands may vary by region; substitute a similar product.

MEXI DIP

1 16-ounce can refried beans
1 cup Heinz Tomato Ketchup
1 cup shredded Cheddar cheese
2 tablespoons diced canned green chiles
1 teaspoon hot pepper sauce
1 cup dairy sour cream

1. In a medium saucepan, combine beans, ketchup, cheese, chiles and hot pepper sauce. Cook on medium heat until cheese is melted, about 3 minutes, stirring occasionally.
2. Stir in sour cream; heat gently until warmed. Do not boil. Makes 4 cups.

EL MONTEREY
Fiesta Platter with
Sun-Dried Tomato Dip ▲

To create your fiesta, we recommend the following El Monterey Taquitos:

El Monterey* Shredded Chicken Corn Taquitos
El Monterey* Shredded Steak Corn Taquitos
El Monterey* Chicken and Cheese Flour Taquitos
El Monterey* Steak and Cheese Flour Taquitos
Mexican Grill* Chicken and Cheese Flour Taquitos

SUN-DRIED TOMATO DIP
$1/4$ cup sun-dried tomatoes
Balsamic vinegar
$1/3$ cup sour cream
$1/3$ cup mayonnaise
$1/3$ cup plain yogurt
2 garlic cloves, finely minced
1 tablespoon chopped fresh basil, or 1 teaspoon dried
$1/4$ cup green olives, chopped

1. Place tomatoes in a small bowl and add vinegar to just cover.
Let soak for about 1 hour.

2. Remove tomatoes from vinegar and drain well. Chop fine and
mix with sour cream, mayonnaise, yogurt, garlic, basil and olives.

3. Refrigerate until ready to serve. Makes 16 servings.

* Brands may vary by region; substitute a similar product.

DON MIGUEL MEXICAN FOODS
Avocado and Garlic Dip ▲

1 ripe avocado, chopped
1 tablespoon sour cream
1 garlic clove, crushed and mashed to a paste
Juice of $1/2$ lime
2 green onions, chopped
Salt and pepper to taste
$1/4$ teaspoon red pepper flakes

Place all ingredients in a bowl and stir to blend. Serve with your favorite
Don Miguel Mexican Foods item. Makes 2-4 servings.

Tip: Try this delicious dip with any of our Don Miguel Mexican Foods*
such as Beef, Chicken Chipotle or Garlic Chicken Flautas; Chicken or Beef
Mini Tacos or Taquitos; Lean Ole Variety Pack Burritos; and Fiesta Appetizer
Platter. It can be served with hot or cold items, which makes it perfect for
any kind of gathering.

* Brands may vary by region; substitute a similar product.

GENERAL MILLS
Crescent-Wrapped Brie ▲

1 8-ounce can Pillsbury* refrigerated crescent dinner rolls
1 8-ounce round natural Brie cheese
1 egg, beaten

1. Preheat oven to 350°F. Unroll dough. Separate crosswise into 2 sections. Pat dough and firmly press perforations to seal, forming 2 squares. Place 1 square on an ungreased cookie sheet. Place cheese round on center of dough.
2. With a small cookie or canapé cutter, cut 1 shape from each corner of remaining square of dough; set cutouts aside.

3. Place remaining square on top of cheese round. Press dough evenly around cheese; fold bottom edges over top edges. Gently stretch dough evenly around cheese; press to seal completely. Brush with beaten egg. Top with cutouts; brush again with beaten egg.
4. Bake for 20-24 minutes, or until golden brown. Cool for 15 minutes before serving. Makes 12 servings.

Brands may vary by region; substitute a similar product.

General Mills

SUNSET
Hot Cucumber and Artichoke Dip
by Mastronardi Produce ▼

¹/₂ **cup mayonnaise**

¹/₂ **cup grated Parmesan cheese**

¹/₄ **cup chopped green onion**

1 14-ounce can artichoke hearts, drained and chopped

1 Sunset seedless cucumber, chopped

1 garlic clove, crushed, optional

Crackers or rye bread

1. Heat oven to 350°F.

2. Mix mayonnaise and cheese in a small bowl. Stir in green onion, artichoke hearts, cucumber and garlic. Spoon into a 1-quart casserole.

3. Cover and bake for 20-25 minutes, or until hot. Serve warm with crackers. Makes 8 servings.

Appetizers █

MARINE HARVEST
Salmon Salad ▲

1 7-ounce can Kirkland Signature salmon, drained
2 tablespoons mayonnaise, or according to taste
2 tablespoons finely chopped celery
1 tablespoon finely chopped onion
1 tablespoon finely chopped red bell pepper, optional
2 teaspoons finely chopped fresh dill
Crackers or toast points

1. Flake salmon into a bowl; mix with mayonnaise, celery, onion, bell pepper and dill.

2. Serve salad on fine crackers or toast points. Makes 6 servings.

MARINE HARVEST
Deviled Eggs with Smoked Salmon ▲

8 hard-boiled large eggs, peeled and cut in half lengthwise
3 tablespoons mayonnaise
1 tablespoon sour cream
2 teaspoons Dijon mustard
$1/2$ teaspoon fresh lemon juice
2 teaspoons finely chopped fresh dill
4 packed tablespoons finely minced Kirkland Signature
    smoked salmon
Salt and pepper
Dill sprigs

1. Remove yolks from eggs and mash with mayonnaise, sour cream, mustard and lemon juice. Stir in dill and smoked salmon. Add salt and pepper to taste.

2. Spoon the mixture into the egg whites. Garnish each deviled egg with a fresh dill sprig. Chill for at least 1 hour before serving. Makes 8 servings.

MAZZETTA
Shrimp Cocktail ▼

2 lemons
4 quarts water
2 tablespoons kosher salt
4 bay leaves
1 pound Seamazz U-15 thawed raw shell-on shrimp
Prepared cocktail sauce
Mint leaves, for garnish

1. Cut 1 lemon in half and place in a large pot with the water, salt and bay leaves. Bring to a steady boil.

2. Add shrimp and cook for 2-3 minutes. Shrimp is done when the meat is opaque and firm to the touch.

3. Drain shrimp and run under cold water. Peel and devein. Rinse and store shrimp in a covered dish in the refrigerator until ready to serve. Shrimp can be prepared 24 hours in advance.

4. Cut the remaining lemon in wedges. Serve the shrimp with your favorite cocktail sauce. Garnish with lemon wedges and mint leaves. Makes 4 servings.

Mazzetta Company, LLC ®

Appetizers **I**

OKAMI
Sushi Dipping Sauces ▼

Use these dipping sauces with Okami Sushi, available in your local Costco deli:*

OKAMI GARI SAUCE

$^1/_2$ **cup sake**
$^1/_2$ **cup soy sauce**
$^1/_4$ **cup sugar**
$^1/_4$ **cup grated white radish**
1 teaspoon grated fresh ginger

1. In a small saucepan, combine sake, soy and sugar.
2. Simmer over low heat for 3-5 minutes, or until sugar dissolves. Transfer to a bowl and chill.
3. Stir in radish and ginger. Makes 8 servings.

Brands may vary by region; substitute a similar product.

OKAMI WASABI SAUCE

$^1/_2$ **cup wasabi powder**
1 tablespoon mirin
1 teaspoon sugar
$^1/_2$ **cup water**
$^1/_2$ **cup peanut oil**

1. In a bowl, whisk together wasabi, mirin and sugar.
2. Add water until a loose puree forms. Whisk in oil. Makes 8 servings.

OKAMI PONZU SAUCE

2 tablespoons lime juice
2 tablespoons soy sauce
2 tablespoons water
1 tablespoon rice vinegar
1 teaspoon minced ginger
2 teaspoons sugar

Combine ingredients in a blender and puree. Makes 4 servings.

FOXY FOODS
Southwestern Shrimp Dip in Lettuce Bowl with Crudités

1 head Foxy* iceberg lettuce
1/2 pound cooked bay shrimp, rinsed and well drained
1/2 cup finely chopped red bell pepper
1/2 cup prepared salsa (medium heat)
1/2 cup canned niblet corn, drained
1/2 cup chopped green onions
2 tablespoons chopped fresh parsley
1/2 cup mayonnaise
1/3 cup dairy sour cream
1/2 teaspoon lemon juice
Vegetable crudités: celery sticks, broccoli and cauliflower florets, carrot sticks, etc.
Crackers

1. Trim a 1-inch slice from core end of lettuce head. Stand lettuce head on a flat surface. With a paring knife, cut out the center, leaving a 1/2-inch-thick shell. Remove lettuce from the center; reserve for another use. Wrap lettuce "bowl" in moist paper toweling and chill.
2. In a bowl, combine shrimp, bell pepper, salsa, corn, green onions, parsley, mayonnaise, sour cream and lemon juice. Cover and chill for at least 1 hour.
3. Place the lettuce bowl on a platter. Spoon dip into lettuce bowl. Arrange crudités and crackers around lettuce bowl. Makes 12 servings.

Brands may vary by region; substitute a similar product.

TANIMURA & ANTLE
Romaine BBQ Teasers

1 cup diced cooked chicken (approximately one 8-ounce boneless chicken breast)
1/2 cup diced sharp Cheddar cheese
1/2 cup chopped red onion
3-4 tablespoons barbecue sauce
Salt
1 head Tanimura & Antle* romaine hearts

1. Combine chicken, cheese, onion and barbecue sauce in a small bowl; season to taste with salt.
2. Remove large leaves from romaine heart; reserve for other uses. Arrange inner leaves on a large platter and fill centers with chicken mixture. Cut leaves in half crosswise, if necessary. Makes 4-6 servings.
Creative ideas: Try leftover rotisserie chicken or tuna salad in romaine hearts for a convenient change of pace.
For vegetarian Mediterranean Teasers, combine 1 1/2 cups diced tomatoes with 1 tablespoon olive oil, 1 teaspoon balsamic vinegar and 1/2 teaspoon dried basil (or 1 tablespoon chopped fresh basil). Season to taste with salt and pepper.

Brands may vary by region; substitute a similar product.

NEW YORK STYLE SAUSAGE
Polenta Pie with Sausage, Spinach and Sun-Dried Tomatoes

POLENTA CRUST

3 cups water

1 teaspoon salt

1 cup yellow cornmeal

1 cup shredded sharp
  Cheddar cheese

FILLING

8 ounces New York Style Sausage*
  Italian sausage

2 green onions, chopped

4 garlic cloves, chopped

1/4 teaspoon salt

1 1/2 ounces (1/2 bag) Sonoma
  dried tomato halves, blanched
  and thinly sliced

1 10-ounce package frozen
  chopped spinach, thawed,
  squeezed dry

1 cup shredded mozzarella cheese

Italian parsley, chopped,
  for garnish

1. To prepare crust, bring water and salt to a boil in a large saucepan. Reduce heat to medium-low. Sprinkle in cornmeal, whisking constantly with a wooden spoon to prevent lumps. Boil gently for 10-15 minutes, stirring often, until thick but pourable. Stir in Cheddar and cook until cheese melts. Pour into a 10-inch pie plate. Set aside.

2. Preheat oven to 400°F.

3. Prepare filling by spraying a large skillet with nonstick spray. Remove sausages from casing and sauté with onions, garlic, salt and dried tomatoes for 10-12 minutes, or until sausage is browned.

4. Assemble pie by spreading spinach evenly over polenta. Top with filling; sprinkle with mozzarella. Bake for 15-20 minutes, or until heated thoroughly. Garnish with parsley. Serve hot. Makes 6-8 servings.

Brands may vary by region; substitute a similar product.

GRACE BAKING
Smoked Turkey Paté Gondola

1 loaf Grace Baking* Pugliese artisan bread

1 pound precooked smoked turkey

6 ounces cream cheese, softened

2 tablespoons mayonnaise

2 tablespoons chopped fresh dill

1 cup chopped red onion

2 tablespoons capers

1 teaspoon hot pepper sauce

2 cups finely chopped Belgian endive

1. Cut off the top of the bread loaf. Hollow out the loaf. Cut the top into slices for serving.

2. Cut smoked turkey into chunks. Place in a food processor and pulse until finely chopped.

3. Place turkey in a large bowl; fold in cream cheese, mayonnaise, dill, onion, capers, hot pepper sauce and Belgian endive.

4. Fill the hollowed-out loaf with the mixture. Serve with reserved slices of bread. Makes 16 servings.

Brands may vary by region; substitute a similar product.

GRACE BAKING

CARDILE BROTHERS
Famous Sausage-Stuffed Mushrooms ▼

12 ounces breakfast sausage
18 Cardile Brothers* large white mushrooms
2 8-ounce packages cream cheese, softened
3/4 cup dry bread crumbs
3/4 cup red wine
Bacon bits, optional

1. Preheat oven to 325°F.

2. Cook sausage in a large, deep skillet over medium-high heat, stirring and breaking up sausage with a fork, until evenly browned. Drain and set aside.

3. Clean mushrooms. Remove, chop and reserve the stems.

4. In a medium bowl, gently mix the chopped mushroom stems, cream cheese and bread crumbs. Stir in the sausage and 1/4 cup red wine. For a different taste, add bacon bits.

5. Spoon the sausage mixture into the mushroom caps. Transfer to a large baking dish and cover with the remaining red wine.

6. Bake for 25-30 minutes, or until lightly browned. Makes 6 servings.

Brands may vary by region; substitute a similar product.

Appetizers |

ORIGINAL NUT HOUSE/
ANN'S HOUSE OF NUTS
Kathy Casey's Chili-Roasted Cashews ▼

1 egg white
1 tablespoon water
1 pound (about 3 1/2 cups) Kirkland Signature Whole
   Fancy Indian Cashews
1/3 cup sugar
1 tablespoon mild chili powder
2 teaspoons ground cumin
2 teaspoons kosher salt
1/2 teaspoon cayenne pepper

1. Preheat oven to 250°F.
2. In a medium bowl, whisk egg white with water until foamy. Add cashews and toss to coat. Transfer the nuts to a strainer, shake, and let drain for at least 2 minutes.
3. In a large bowl, mix together sugar, chili powder, cumin, salt and cayenne. Add the nuts and toss to coat thoroughly.
4. On a large baking sheet with sides, spread the nuts out in a single layer. Bake for 40 minutes. Stir the nuts with a spatula and spread them out again. Bake 20-30 minutes longer, or until dry.
5. Loosen the nuts from the baking sheet but do not remove them. Cool to room temperature. Be sure to let the nuts cool completely and become crisp. Store in an airtight container at room temperature for up to 2 weeks. Makes 3 1/2 cups.

Recipe provided by Kathy Casey Food Studios.

KIRKLAND
Signature

Easy Cooking The Costco Way

KEYSTONE
Skewered Sweet Onions with Shrimp ▲

3 pounds shrimp (21/25 or 26/30 count)

2 pineapples

20 skewers

3 Keystone* sweet onions, cut in chunks

2 red bell peppers, cut in chunks

3 tablespoons extra-virgin olive oil, divided

1/4 cup Chesapeake Bay-style seafood seasoning

1/2 pound butter

2 lemons

2 limes

2 garlic cloves, minced

1/2 cup chopped fresh parsley

1/2 cup chopped fresh basil

1 tablespoon fresh thyme

1. Steam 1 pound shrimp. Peel 1 pineapple and cut into chunks.

2. Peel remaining 2 pounds shrimp; thread on skewers with pineapple chunks, onions and peppers; thread any remaining vegetables on skewers.

3. Brush with 2 tablespoons oil and sprinkle with seafood seasoning. Grill skewers, basting with remaining oil; keep warm.

4. Melt butter in a saucepan over low heat. Add the juice and grated peel of 1 lemon and 1 lime, garlic and herbs; keep warm.

5. Brush warm sauce on the cooked skewers and pierce the whole pineapple with the skewers. Place remaining vegetables and steamed shrimp around the pineapple. Top with sauce, lemon juice and lime juice. Makes 10 servings.

Brands may vary by region; substitute a similar product.

ConAgra
TexMexiMix ▲

12 cups popped ACT II Microwave Popcorn, butter flavor (about 3 bags)

4 cups slightly crushed tortilla chips

2 2.8-ounce cans french-fried onions

1/4 cup butter

1 1 1/4-ounce package dry taco seasoning mix

1. Preheat oven to 350°F.

2. Combine popcorn with tortilla chips and onions in a large bowl.

3. Melt butter with half of the taco seasoning mix in a medium saucepan over low heat. Pour over the popcorn mixture, tossing gently to coat.

4. Spread on a large baking sheet. Bake for 3-5 minutes. Pour into a large serving bowl. Sprinkle remaining taco seasoning mix over the popcorn, tossing to coat evenly. Serve immediately or store in an airtight container. Makes 16 cups.

Salads and Soups

Hass Avocado and Blueberry Fruit Salad ◀

DRESSING

2 teaspoons honey
1 ¹/₂ teaspoons Dijon mustard
¹/₂ teaspoon ground cinnamon
¹/₄ cup apple cider vinegar
¹/₂ cup walnut oil
¹/₈ teaspoon salt
¹/₈ teaspoon freshly ground black pepper

1 large, ripe Hass avocado, pitted, peeled and sliced
1 cup fresh blueberries, rinsed, picked over and well drained
1 cup diced fresh apple
1 cup diced fresh mango
8 cups mixed baby greens
¹/₄ cup chopped chives or green onion
¹/₄ cup walnuts, toasted, coarsely chopped

1. To make the dressing, mix honey, mustard and cinnamon in a medium bowl to make a smooth paste. Whisk in vinegar. Add oil in a thin stream, whisking constantly until dressing is creamy. Stir in salt and pepper; taste and adjust seasoning. Makes about ³/₄ cup.
2. Place avocado, blueberries, apple and mango in a medium bowl and toss with 4 tablespoons dressing; set aside.
3. Place salad greens in a large bowl and toss with ¹/₄ cup dressing; distribute evenly on 8 salad plates. Top with dressed avocado/fruit mixture. Sprinkle with chives and toasted walnuts. Remainder of salad dressing can be refrigerated for later use. Makes 8 servings.

Presented by the California Avocado Commission, Chilean Avocado Importers Association, Calavo Growers, Index Fresh, West Pak Avocado, Mission Produce, Giumarra and Del Rey Avocado.

DNE WORLD FRUIT Citrus Tossed Salad ▲

³/₄ cup frozen Florida orange juice concentrate, thawed
¹/₄ cup vinegar
¹/₄ cup olive oil
¹/₄ cup water
¹/₄ teaspoon pepper
6 cups torn mixed salad greens
3 Florida oranges or 2 Florida grapefruits, peeled, sectioned and seeded
1 ¹/₂ cups julienne strips of peeled jicama
1 medium red onion, sliced and separated into rings

1. In a jar, combine orange juice concentrate, vinegar, olive oil, water and pepper; cover and shake well. Chill for up to 1 week. Before using, let stand at room temperature for 15 minutes, then shake well.
2. In a large salad bowl, combine salad greens, orange or grapefruit sections, jicama and onion rings. Drizzle with ¹/₃ cup of the vinaigrette; toss. Serve at once. Makes 6 servings.

World Fruit Sales

NEWSTAR
Savory Young & Tender Apple Spinach Salad ▲

1 pound NewStar* Young & Tender Spinach, chopped

2 large or 3 small apples, cored and diced

1/3 cup chopped walnuts, toasted

1/3 cup thinly sliced red onion

1 tablespoon Dijon mustard

2 teaspoons lemon juice

1/2 teaspoon sugar

2/3 cup olive oil

Salt and pepper

1. In a large bowl, combine spinach, apples, walnuts and onion.

2. In a small bowl, whisk together mustard, lemon juice and sugar. Slowly whisk in olive oil. Season to taste with salt and pepper.

3. Add dressing to taste to the salad and toss well. Makes 6 servings.

Brands may vary by region; substitute a similar product.

VINTAGE PRESS RESTAURANTE
Grape Salad with Pecans and Roquefort Cheese ▲

3/4 cup Kirkland Signature Pecan Halves

1 egg white, beaten

1/4 cup brown sugar

1 shallot, diced

1/2 cup balsamic vinegar

3/4 cup olive oil

1/4 cup chopped fresh basil

Salt and freshly ground pepper

6 cups assorted baby greens

2 cups Stevco* seedless grapes

4 ounces Roquefort cheese, crumbled

1/2 cup sliced sun-dried tomatoes

6 thin slices prosciutto

1. Preheat oven to 350°F. Coat pecans with beaten egg white; toss with brown sugar. Place on a baking sheet and bake for 10 minutes, or until golden. Remove from oven and let cool.

2. Whisk together shallots and vinegar. Slowly whisk in olive oil. Add basil and season to taste with salt and pepper.

3. Combine greens, grapes, Roquefort and tomatoes in a salad bowl. Add dressing to lightly coat the greens. Place on chilled plates; top each serving with a slice of prosciutto and pecans. Makes 6 servings.

Recipe created by Chef David Vartanian of the Vintage Press Restaurante, Visalia, California.
Brands may vary by region; substitute a similar product.

BOSKOVICH FARMS
Spinach Salad with Strawberries ▼

6 cups Boskovich Farms* Fresh 'N' Quick Spinach
1 pint fresh strawberries, stems removed, halved
1/2 cup sugar
2 tablespoons toasted sesame seeds
1 tablespoon poppy seeds
2 teaspoons finely chopped sweet onion
1/2 teaspoon white wine Worcestershire sauce
1/4 teaspoon paprika
1/2 cup vegetable oil
1/4 cup balsamic vinegar

1. Toss spinach and strawberries in a salad bowl.

2. In a blender, combine sugar, sesame seeds, poppy seeds, onion, Worcestershire sauce and paprika. Add oil and vinegar slowly, blending until smooth and thickened.

3. Pour dressing over salad and serve immediately. Makes 4 servings.

* Brands may vary by region; substitute a similar product.

TANIMURA & ANTLE
Blue Cheese Iceberg Wedges ▾

1 head Tanimura & Antle* iceberg lettuce
1 ½ cups blue cheese or Roquefort salad dressing
1 large red apple or red pear, cored and cubed
⅓ cup diced sharp Cheddar cheese
¼ cup toasted walnut pieces or slivered almonds

1. Remove core and outer leaf from lettuce. Cut head into 6 wedges and place 1 wedge on each salad plate.

2. Drizzle ¼ cup dressing over each wedge. Top with fruit, cheese and nuts. Add more dressing if desired. Makes 6 servings.

Creative ideas:

1. For Creamy Ranch Iceberg Wedges, top with slices of cucumber, matchstick or shredded carrots and cherry tomato halves. Drizzle with Creamy Ranch dressing.

2. For Thousand Island Iceberg Wedges, top with cherry tomato halves, sliced green or black olives and sliced green onions. Drizzle with Thousand Island dressing.

*Brands may vary by region; substitute a similar product.

YAKIMA-ROCHE FRUIT
Apple and Pear Salad ▲

3 heads Belgian endive
3 cups assorted torn salad greens
2 cups julienned apples
2 cups julienned pears
1 cup crumbled Gorgonzola cheese
1 cup pecan halves, toasted
1/2 cup olive oil
1/2 cup walnut oil
1/2 cup tarragon vinegar
1 tablespoon frozen orange juice concentrate, thawed
Salt and freshly ground pepper

1. Place 3-4 spears of Belgian endive in a sunburst pattern on each of 6-8 chilled salad plates. Place salad greens on the endive. Casually arrange apples and pears on the greens. Sprinkle lightly with Gorgonzola and pecans.
2. In a bowl, whisk together olive oil, walnut oil, vinegar, orange juice concentrate, and salt and pepper to taste. Spoon the dressing over the salad to taste. Makes 6-8 servings.

Tip: Add sliced smoked chicken breast for a substantial main course.

METZ FRESH
Spinach, Avocado and Orange Salad ▲

4-5 cups Metz Fresh* spinach leaves
6-8 tiny red potatoes, cooked and cooled
4 radishes, trimmed and thinly sliced
2 tablespoons balsamic vinegar
5 tablespoons extra-virgin olive oil
1 1/2 teaspoons sugar
1/4 teaspoon minced garlic
1 1/2 teaspoons grated orange peel
Salt and pepper
2 oranges, peeled, sliced and sectioned
2 avocados, peeled and sliced

1. In a large bowl, combine spinach, potatoes and radishes.
2. In a glass measuring cup, whisk together vinegar and oil; add sugar, garlic, grated orange peel, and salt and pepper to taste.
3. Pour the dressing over the salad and gently toss. Top with orange and avocado slices. Makes 4-5 servings.

Brands may vary by region; substitute a similar product.

DOMEX
Crunchy Three-Apple Salad

1 cup canned pineapple tidbits in juice
2 medium Washington Gala apples, cored and diced
1 medium Washington Red Delicious apple, cored and diced
1 medium Washington Granny Smith apple, cored and diced
2-3 tablespoons lemon juice
4 ounces cream cheese, softened
1 cup whipped topping
$^1/_2$ cup coarsely chopped pecans
1 cup miniature marshmallows

1. Drain pineapple in a small colander, reserving the juice. Sprinkle apples with lemon juice to preserve color.
2. Place cream cheese in a bowl and whisk in reserved pineapple juice until smooth. Stir in whipped topping. Gently mix in pineapple, apples, pecans and marshmallows. Cover and refrigerate until ready to serve. Makes 12 servings.

BOUNTY FRESH/LEGEND PRODUCE
Cantaloupe, Pineapple and Mango Salad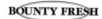

1 large ripe mango, finely diced
$^1/_2$ small red onion, finely diced
1 medium jalapeño pepper, minced
$^1/_2$ cup minced cantaloupe
3 tablespoons chopped fresh cilantro
2 tablespoons chopped fresh parsley
2 tablespoons lemon juice
1 tablespoon extra-virgin olive oil
1 teaspoon minced garlic
1 teaspoon honey
1 teaspoon kosher salt
1 large pineapple, peeled, cored and cut in thin rings
1 cup watercress

1. In a medium stainless-steel bowl, combine mango, onion, jalapeño, cantaloupe, cilantro, parsley, lemon juice, olive oil, garlic, honey and salt. Mix well and cover. Set aside for 1 hour to let the flavors blend.
2. Arrange 3 pineapple rings on each plate. Top with watercress and fruit salsa. Makes 4 servings.
Chef's tip: To make this salad a little more dynamic, grill the pineapple and serve it warm with chilled salsa.
Recipe created by Chef Allen Susser.

DOLE
Tropical Fruit and Walnut Salad ▼

6 cups Dole* Classic Iceberg Salad

1 20-ounce can Dole* Pineapple Chunks, drained,
    or 1 1/2 cups Dole* Fresh Pineapple Chunks

1 cup Dole* red grapes, cut in half

2 Dole* bananas, sliced

1/2 cup (2 ounces) crumbled feta cheese

1/2 cup coarsely chopped walnuts, toasted

2/3 cup ranch dressing or balsamic vinaigrette

1. In a salad bowl, combine salad greens, pineapple, grapes, bananas, feta and walnuts.

2. Add dressing and toss salad. Serve immediately. Makes 6-8 servings.

Tip: To serve as a main-dish salad, add 2 cups cubed cooked chicken to the mixture.

* Brands may vary by region; substitute a similar product.

EARTHBOUND FARM
Mixed Baby Greens with Apples,
Bacon and Stilton ▲

1 teaspoon finely
   minced shallot

1 teaspoon Dijon mustard

$1/4$ cup balsamic vinegar

$3/4$ cup extra-virgin olive oil

$1/2$ teaspoon salt

$1/4$ teaspoon freshly ground
   black pepper

8 ounces Earthbound Farm*
   Organic Mixed Baby Greens

1 cup walnut halves, toasted

8 strips crispy cooked bacon, crumbled

4 ounces Stilton cheese
   (or other bleu cheese), crumbled

2 small Gala or Fuji apples, cored and
   thinly sliced

1. To prepare vinaigrette, combine shallot, mustard, vinegar, oil, salt and pepper in a jar and shake vigorously.

2. Place mixed baby greens in a large bowl, add vinaigrette to taste and toss. Refrigerate any unused vinaigrette.

3. Divide salad among 8 plates and sprinkle each serving with toasted walnuts, crumbled bacon and Stilton. Garnish salads with apple slices and serve immediately. Makes 8 servings.

Brands may vary by region; substitute a similar product.

ANDY BOY
Ultimate Caesar Salad

2 Andy Boy* romaine hearts, leaves separated and torn
1 egg, lightly beaten
2 garlic cloves, crushed
3 tablespoons fresh lemon juice
2 teaspoons Dijon mustard
1 2 1/2- to 3-ounce can finely minced anchovy fillets, drained
1/2 cup olive oil
2 hard-boiled eggs, peeled and quartered
1/2 cup freshly grated Parmesan cheese
3/4 cup pumpernickel croutons
Freshly ground pepper

1. Rinse romaine hearts and dry. Wrap in paper towels and refrigerate for several hours to crisp leaves.

2. Whisk the raw egg, garlic, lemon juice, Dijon, anchovies and oil together and pour into the bottom of a salad bowl.

3. Add the lettuce and hard-boiled eggs and toss thoroughly with the dressing. Add Parmesan and toss again. Sprinkle with croutons and a generous sweep of freshly ground pepper. Makes 4 servings.

* Brands may vary by region; substitute a similar product.

BC HOT HOUSE
Marinated Tomatoes and Cucumbers ▲

2 pounds BC Hot House* Campari tomatoes
2 BC Hot House* long English cucumbers
1 BC Hot House* yellow sweet bell pepper
3/4 cup oil
1/2 cup red wine vinegar
1 teaspoon chopped fresh oregano
1/2 teaspoon fresh thyme leaves
1/2 teaspoon sugar
1 teaspoon salt
1/4 teaspoon garlic powder
2 teaspoons chopped fresh parsley

1. Coarsely chop tomatoes, cucumbers and yellow pepper. Arrange alternately in a shallow dish.
2. Combine oil, vinegar, oregano, thyme, sugar, salt and garlic powder in a jar. Shake until well mixed; pour over vegetables.
3. Marinate for 3-4 hours, basting occasionally. Drain vegetables; sprinkle with parsley. Makes 4-6 servings.

* Brands may vary by region; substitute a similar product.

POCKET MEALS
Creamy Italian Vinaigrette ▲

1/4 cup fresh lemon juice or cider vinegar
3/4 teaspoon salt
1/4 teaspoon black pepper
3/4 cup olive oil
1 egg white
Salad greens
Pocket Meals Pepperoni Pizza

1. Combine lemon juice or vinegar, salt and pepper in a blender or food processor.
2. With the machine running, add olive oil 1 tablespoon at a time.
3. Beat egg white with a whisk until frothy. Whisk into the vinaigrette. Makes 1 cup.
4. Toss vinaigrette with your favorite salad greens. Serve with Pocket Meals Pepperoni Pizza (flavor may vary by region).

Nestlé

OSO SWEET
Hot and Sweet Coleslaw

³/₄ cup cider vinegar

³/₄ cup olive oil

¹/₂ cup sugar

1 garlic clove, minced

Salt

1 medium head red cabbage (about 2 pounds),
  cored and finely shredded

1 OSO Sweet onion, halved and thinly sliced

2 serrano chiles, finely chopped

Freshly ground pepper

1. In a large bowl, whisk together vinegar, oil, sugar, garlic and 1 teaspoon salt. Set aside until sugar dissolves.

2. Add cabbage, onion and chiles; toss gently to mix. Taste, adding salt and pepper as needed. Serve at once, or refrigerate, covered, for up to 24 hours. Makes 6-8 servings.

SEA WATCH
Amazing Clam and Crab Salad
Stuffed Avocados

¹/₂ cup finely diced red bell pepper

¹/₂ cup finely diced green bell pepper

¹/₂ cup quartered and thinly sliced red onion

¹/₂ cup finely diced celery

¹/₂ cup peeled and shredded carrot

¹/₄ cup fresh lime juice

2 teaspoons ground cumin

¹/₄ cup finely chopped fresh cilantro

1 cup mayonnaise

1 51-ounce can Sea Watch* Chopped Sea Clams, well drained

1 pound jumbo lump crabmeat, well drained

6 ripe avocados, pitted and halved

3 limes, quartered, for garnish

1. In a large bowl, combine bell peppers, onion, celery, carrot, lime juice, cumin, cilantro and mayonnaise; mix well. Gently fold in chopped clams and crabmeat. Cover and refrigerate for at least 1 hour to chill and allow flavors to develop.

2. Scoop ¹/₂ cup of clam and crab salad into each avocado half. Serve with lime wedges. Makes 12 servings.

Brands may vary by region; substitute a similar product.

BelGioioso Cheese
Fresh Mozzarella Salad ▼

1 pound BelGioioso Fresh Mozzarella
2 tablespoons extra-virgin olive oil
1 cup bread crumbs
$^1/_4$ cup ground nuts
3 cups mixed fresh salad greens
1 tablespoon balsamic vinegar
3 slices prosciutto, chopped
$^1/_2$ cup kalamata olives
$^1/_2$ cup chopped fresh tomato

1. Preheat oven to 425°F.
2. Cut mozzarella into eight $^1/_2$-inch-thick slices. Marinate in olive oil for 1-2 minutes.
3. Combine bread crumbs and ground nuts. Dredge marinated cheese slices in bread crumb/nut mixture; place on a baking sheet. Bake for 3-4 minutes, or until warm.
4. Put salad greens in a bowl and toss with vinegar. Place salad greens on plates. Top with warm mozzarella and garnish with prosciutto, olives and tomatoes. Makes 4 servings.

TOP BRASS
Grilled Red Potato Salad

4 pounds California Fresh Top Brass* red potatoes,
    scrubbed and cooked until tender, drained and halved

$1/2$ cup olive oil, divided

Salt and pepper

$3/4$ pound bacon

1 large red onion, thinly sliced

$1/4$ cup white wine vinegar

1 tablespoon sugar

$1/4$ cup chopped fresh parsley

1 cup crumbled blue cheese

1. Preheat grill.

2. Toss potatoes in a bowl with $1/4$ cup olive oil and salt and pepper to taste. Grill potatoes for 3 minutes on each side; set aside.

3. Cook bacon in a skillet until browned and crisp. Remove from the pan, cool and then crumble.

4. Remove all but 2 tablespoons of bacon fat from the pan. Add onions and cook over medium heat until soft, 5-6 minutes. Stir in $1/4$ cup olive oil, vinegar and sugar; cook until sugar is dissolved.

5. Place potatoes in a large bowl. Pour onions over potatoes; add bacon, parsley, and salt and pepper to taste. Toss to mix. Sprinkle with crumbled blue cheese. Makes 8 servings.

Brands may vary by region; substitute a similar product.

L&M
Nature's Delight Baked Potato Salad

8 L&M* Nature's Delight baking potatoes, cooked, peeled and diced

1 pound Velveeta or similar cheese, cubed (light works fine)

1 cup real mayonnaise

$1/2$ cup chopped onions

Salt and pepper

$1/2$ pound bacon, fried and crumbled

1. Preheat oven to 325°F.

2. In a large bowl, combine potatoes, cheese, mayonnaise, onions, and salt and pepper to taste. Place in a 9-by-13-inch glass baking dish. Top with crumbled bacon.

3. Bake, uncovered, for 1 hour. Do not overbake, as it tends to separate. Makes 12 servings.

This recipe was submitted by the Baskett family of L&M Companies in Raleigh, North Carolina.
* Brands may vary by region; substitute a similar product.

L&M
COMPANIES, INC.®

CELLO
New Wave Salad with Shredded Italian Parmesan, Grana Padano

2 cups fresh basil leaves
1 tablespoon olive oil
8 ounces fettuccine
1 $^1/_2$ cups vinaigrette
1 pound green beans, trimmed
6 ripe plum tomatoes, each cut into 8 pieces
2 cups kalamata or other black olives
2 tablespoons chopped fresh parsley
4 ounces shredded Cello Italian Parmesan, Grana Padano

1. Arrange basil leaves in a small stack and roll up lengthwise; slice diagonally into slivers.
2. Bring a large pot of water to a boil. Add oil and fettuccine and cook at a rolling boil until just tender. Drain, rinse under cold water, drain, and place in a large bowl. Add $^1/_2$ cup vinaigrette and toss.
3. Bring a large saucepan of water to a boil; add beans. Simmer until just tender, 5-8 minutes. Drain, rinse under cold water, and drain.
4. Place pasta in a serving bowl. Cover with tomatoes and green beans, then olives, slivered basil and parsley. Pour the remaining vinaigrette over the salad. Sprinkle with Grana Padano and toss well. Makes 8 servings.

arthur schuman inc.

SUN-MAID RAISIN
Broccoli Pasta Toss

1 cup small broccoli florets
1 $^1/_4$ cups cooked shell pasta
$^1/_2$ cup Sun-Maid Natural Raisins
$^1/_3$ cup chopped red onion
$^1/_4$ cup chopped red bell pepper
$^1/_3$ cup reduced-calorie mayonnaise
1 tablespoon cider vinegar
$^1/_2$ teaspoon sugar
Salt and pepper

1. In a salad bowl, combine broccoli, pasta, raisins, onion and bell pepper.
2. Whisk together mayonnaise, vinegar and sugar in a small bowl. Pour the dressing over the salad. Add salt and pepper to taste. Gently toss. Makes 4 servings.

AQUA FARMS
Salmon and Clam Soup ▼

2 pounds Kirkland Signature salmon fillets,
    divided into 6 equal pieces

10 garlic cloves, unpeeled

2 tablespoons olive oil

7 cups rich chicken stock

60 small fresh clams in the shell, scrubbed

6 cups loosely packed fresh spinach leaves, cut in 1-inch-wide strips

2 teaspoons (or more) fresh lemon juice

1/8 teaspoon red pepper flakes

Salt and pepper

1 cup chopped fresh tomatoes

1. Preheat oven to 400°F.

2. Wash salmon and pat dry. Arrange salmon, skin side down, and garlic cloves in a single layer in a baking pan. Drizzle with 1 tablespoon of olive oil. Bake, uncovered, for 15-20 minutes, or until salmon has an internal temperature of 140°F. (It will be slightly translucent in the thickest part.) Remember that salmon continues to cook after it is removed from the heat source. Remove salmon to a warming platter.

3. Peel roasted garlic and cut in thin slices. Heat remaining 1 tablespoon olive oil in a large, heavy saucepan. Add garlic and cook over medium heat, stirring frequently, until lightly browned but not burned.

4. Add stock, turn heat to high and bring to a boil. Add clams, cover and check in about 4 minutes. Remove any clams that do not open after 6-8 minutes. Add spinach and cook briefly until it wilts, about 2 minutes. Add lemon juice, red pepper flakes, and salt and pepper to taste.

5. Ladle broth, clams and spinach into soup bowls. (Be watchful for sand.) Nestle a warm piece of salmon in the center of each bowl. Top with a spoonful of chopped tomatoes and serve with French bread. Makes 6 servings.

BEAR CREEK
Skillet Sausage Noodles ▲

8 cups water
2 ²/₃ cups Bear Creek Country Kitchens Chunky Potato Soup Mix
1 pound sliced Italian link sausage
1 large onion, chopped
1 stick (¹/₂ cup) butter
1 teaspoon dried basil
1 cup chopped canned tomatoes
Salt and pepper
Egg noodles, cooked and drained
Grated Cheddar cheese, optional

1. In a large soup pot, bring water to a rolling boil. Whisk in soup mix, reduce heat to medium and simmer for 15 minutes.
2. Brown sausage in a large sauté pan. Once sausage is cooked, add onions, butter and basil. Cook on medium heat until onions are tender; add tomatoes and pour into soup mix. Heat thoroughly, stirring occasionally (approximately 10-15 minutes). Season to taste with salt and pepper.
3. Serve over egg noodles. Sprinkle with grated Cheddar cheese if desired. Makes 10-12 servings.

SUNNY COVE CITRUS
Orange and Carrot Soup ▲

4 tablespoons butter
2 cups chopped yellow onions
2 pounds carrots, peeled and chopped
4 cups chicken stock
1 cup freshly squeezed Sunny Cove orange juice
Salt and pepper
1 tablespoon freshly grated Sunny Cove orange peel
4 tablespoons sour cream
1 teaspoon grated nutmeg

1. Melt butter in a pot, add onions, cover and cook over low heat for 25 minutes, or until tender. Add carrots and stock. Bring to a boil, reduce heat, cover and simmer until carrots are very tender, about 30 minutes.
2. Cool slightly and strain, retaining stock. Pour solids into a food processor and purée. Add 1 cup of the reserved stock and process until smooth.
3. Return the purée to the pot; add orange juice and additional stock (2-3 cups) if needed to reach desired consistency.
4. Season with salt and pepper to taste and grated orange peel. Serve hot or at room temperature. Garnish each serving with a dollop of sour cream and a sprinkle of nutmeg. Makes 4-6 servings.

Sunny Cove

ALPINE FRESH
Roasted Asparagus and Grape Tomato Soup ▲

1 1/2 pounds Alpine Fresh* asparagus, cut in 2-inch slices, plus 12 asparagus tips

2 medium onions, peeled and cut in quarters

40 Alpine Fresh* grape tomatoes

2 tablespoons olive oil

4 cups chicken broth

1/4 teaspoon salt

1/4 teaspoon pepper

1/2 cup half-and-half

6 fresh dill sprigs

1. Preheat oven to 450°F.

2. Place sliced asparagus, fanned-out onion wedges and grape tomatoes in an even layer in a large, shallow roasting pan. Drizzle with olive oil. Roast, uncovered, for 15-20 minutes, or until the vegetables are tender and slightly charred. Remove the tomatoes, chop and set aside.

3. Place half of the other roasted vegetables in a food processor. Add 1 cup of broth and process until smooth. Strain if desired. Transfer to a large saucepan. Repeat with the remaining vegetables. Add as much of the remaining broth to the pan as needed for good consistency, plus salt and pepper.

4. Heat until soup is hot; add half-and-half and heat for another 2 minutes. Ladle into bowls and top each with a spoonful of roasted chopped tomatoes, 2 fresh asparagus tips and a sprig of dill. Makes 6 servings.

Brands may vary by region; substitute a similar product.

TRAPPER'S CREEK
Smoked Kippered King Salmon Chowder ▲

10 strips uncooked bacon, chopped

2 onions, minced

4 stalks celery, minced

3 carrots, finely chopped

5 green onions, finely chopped

3/4 bunch fresh parsley, chopped

1 teaspoon pepper

1 1/2 tablespoons chopped dill weed

6 cups chicken stock

8 red potatoes, diced

4 tablespoons butter

1 cup flour

5 cups milk

1/4 cup lemon juice

1 15 1/4-ounce can corn kernels

1 pound Trapper's Creek* smoked kippered king salmon, flaked

1. Sauté bacon in a large pot with onions, celery, carrots, green onions and parsley. Add pepper, dill, stock and potatoes; simmer until tender.

2. In a small saucepan, melt butter until bubbly. Stir in flour and cook over low heat for 1-2 minutes. Stir into the soup and simmer for 5 minutes.

3. Slowly add milk, stirring constantly; cook over medium heat until slightly thickened. Add lemon juice, corn and salmon. Cook, stirring, at a gentle boil to desired consistency. Makes 8 servings.

Brands may vary by region; substitute a similar product.

Salads and Soups ▌

GIORGIO FOODS
New Low-Fat Mushroom Soup ▲

2 4-ounce cans Brandywine, Giorgio or Pennsylvania Dutch*
   mushrooms, pieces and stems
4 baby carrots, sliced
1 medium rib celery, diced
1 cube chicken or beef bouillon
1/4 teaspoon granulated garlic
1/4 teaspoon onion powder
1/8 teaspoon finely ground black pepper
1/4 teaspoon light soy sauce
1 tablespoon cornstarch
1 cup 2% milk
1/2 tablespoon chopped fresh parsley

1. Drain brine from the mushrooms into a measuring cup. Add enough water to equal 1 1/2 cups. Pour into a saucepan. Add mushrooms, carrots and celery and bring to a boil. Simmer until vegetables are tender, 5-8 minutes.
2. Stir in bouillon cube, granulated garlic, onion powder, pepper and soy sauce.
3. Mix cornstarch with milk; stir into the soup and bring to a boil. Stir in parsley. Makes 3 servings.

Brands may vary by region; substitute a similar product.

MERCER RANCH
Carrot Ginger Soup ▲

7 tablespoons butter, divided
3/4 cup chopped onions
1/3 cup peeled and minced fresh ginger
6 cups chicken broth
2 pounds Mercer Ranch* carrots
1 teaspoon sugar
1 1/2 cups half-and-half
1/4 cup all-purpose flour
1/2 teaspoon ground cinnamon, optional
Salt and pepper
Cream for garnish

1. Melt 4 tablespoons of the butter in a large saucepan over medium heat. Add onions and ginger; cook for 5-7 minutes, or until onions soften. Add broth, carrots and sugar. Lower heat, cover and simmer for 40 minutes.
2. Purée in a blender or food processor (strain if desired). Return to the pan and stir in half-and-half. Cook over low heat for 5 minutes.
3. In a large saucepan, melt the remaining butter and stir in flour; cook over medium heat until bubbly. Slowly add the carrot mixture, stirring constantly until well blended. Season with cinnamon and salt and pepper to taste.
4. Garnish each serving with a swirl of cream. Makes 6 servings.

Brands may vary by region; substitute a similar product.

SWANSON
Sausage and Spinach Soup ▼

Vegetable cooking spray

$1/2$ pound sweet Italian pork sausage, cut in $3/4$-inch pieces

1 32-ounce box Swanson* Chicken Broth or
   Natural Goodness* Chicken Broth (4 cups)

$1/2$ teaspoon dried oregano leaves, crushed

1 medium onion, chopped

1 medium carrot, sliced

2 cups coarsely chopped fresh spinach leaves

1. Spray a large saucepan with cooking spray and heat over medium-high for 1 minute. Add sausage and cook until browned, stirring often. Pour off fat.

2. Add broth, oregano, onion and carrot. Bring to a boil. Cover and cook over low heat for 10 minutes, or until vegetables are tender.

3. Stir in spinach and cook for 1 minute. Makes 5 servings.
Preparation time: 5 minutes. Cooking time: 20 minutes.

Brands may vary by region; substitute a similar product.

Side Dishes

WISCONSIN POTATO GROWERS
Parmesan Potato Wedges ◀

4 large Healthy Grown* russet potatoes, washed and drained

$^1/_4$ cup vegetable oil

$^2/_3$ cup grated Parmesan cheese

$^1/_2$ teaspoon salt

$^1/_2$ teaspoon freshly ground black pepper

4 teaspoons garlic powder

2 teaspoons dried thyme, crushed

1. Preheat oven to 375°F.

2. Cut each potato lengthwise into 6 wedges. Place in a large bowl, add oil and stir until potatoes are well coated.

3. In a small bowl, combine Parmesan, salt, pepper, garlic powder and thyme. Sprinkle mixture on potatoes and stir until potatoes are well coated.

4. Spread potatoes on a greased baking sheet and bake for 35-40 minutes, or until tender and golden brown. Turn potatoes once during baking. Makes 4-6 servings.

* Brands may vary by region; substitute a similar product.

MACK FARMS/SOUTH FLORIDA POTATO GROWERS EXCHANGE
Florida Fresh Potato Bake ▲

6-8 medium new-crop red potatoes

1 large sweet onion

2 garlic cloves, minced

2 tablespoons virgin olive oil

1 tablespoon salt

1 teaspoon black pepper

1. Preheat oven to 425°F.

2. Wash and thinly slice potatoes, leaving skin on. Peel and slice onion.

3. Place potatoes, onions and garlic in a covered casserole dish. Drizzle with olive oil; sprinkle with salt and pepper. Lightly toss together to coat potatoes and onions.

4. Cover casserole and bake for 45-60 minutes, or until potatoes are fork tender. Makes 4 servings.

Tip: For variety, add chopped rosemary, tarragon or parsley.

BASIN GOLD
Potato Pancakes

2 pounds Basin Gold* russet potatoes, peeled and boiled
Juice of 1 lemon
1 tablespoon olive oil
2 garlic cloves, minced
4 eggs
1/2 cup biscuit mix
1 1/2 teaspoons salt
1/2 teaspoon pepper
1 medium onion, chopped
Garnishes: caviar, finely chopped red onion,
    chopped yolks of hard-boiled eggs, sour cream

1. Grate potatoes into a bowl. Stir in lemon juice, olive oil and garlic.
2. Beat eggs in a large bowl; stir in biscuit mix, salt and pepper.
Add onions and the potatoes. Purée in a food processor.
3. Heat a nonstick frying pan on medium-high. Spoon pancake
mixture into the hot skillet in 2-inch rounds. Cook until golden brown;
turn pancakes, press with the spatula, and cook until golden brown.
Serve with garnishes. Makes 48 pancakes.

Serving suggestion: As an alternative for brunch, serve the potato
pancakes with applesauce.

Brands may vary by region; substitute a similar product.

KING PAK
Potato Casserole

6 medium King Pak* white potatoes
6 slices bacon
1 stick (1/2 cup) butter, divided
1 pint sour cream
1 cup shredded Cheddar cheese
1 cup chopped green onions
1/2 cup seasoned bread crumbs

1. Preheat oven to 350°F.
2. Boil potatoes in their skins; peel and grate. Fry and crumble bacon.
Melt half of butter.
3. In a large bowl, combine potatoes, bacon, melted butter, sour cream,
cheese and green onions. Place in a buttered 9-by-13-inch pan. Top with
bread crumbs and dot with remaining butter.
4. Bake for 30 minutes, or until it is heated through and the top is
browned. Makes 12 servings.

Brands may vary by region; substitute a similar product.

CABOT CREAMERY
Macaroni and Cheese ▲

2 cups small elbow macaroni
3 tablespoons butter
3 tablespoons all-purpose flour
$1/4$ teaspoon dry mustard
Pinch of ground red pepper (cayenne)
1 dash Worcestershire sauce
2 cups whole milk, heated
4 cups grated Cabot* Vintage Choice or Private Stock Cheddar, divided
$1/2$ cup buttered bread crumbs

1. Preheat oven to 350°F. Cook and drain macaroni according to package directions.
2. Butter a 2 $1/2$-quart baking dish or coat with nonstick cooking spray.
3. Melt butter in a large saucepan over medium heat. Sprinkle flour into butter and whisk constantly until you have a thick, smooth paste with a nutty aroma, about 5 minutes.
4. Add mustard, red pepper and Worcestershire. Gradually whisk in milk, stirring until sauce thickens and returns to a simmer.
5. Reduce heat to low. Add 3 cups of cheese; stir until melted. Stir in macaroni. Pour into baking dish. Sprinkle with remaining cheese and then crumbs. Bake for 20 minutes, or until golden on top and bubbling throughout. Makes 8 servings.

Brands may vary by region; substitute a similar product.

STAR FINE FOODS
Olive and Ricotta Torte ▲

4 tablespoons extra-virgin olive oil, divided
3 tablespoons plain bread crumbs
2 15-ounce cartons ricotta cheese
$1/2$ cup shredded Parmesan cheese
4 eggs
5 ounces Star* Spanish green olives, drained and sliced
1 14 $1/2$-ounce can diced tomatoes with herbs
3 tablespoons balsamic vinegar
1 tablespoon Star* capers, drained

1. Preheat oven to 350°F.
2. Coat an 8-inch round cake pan with 1 tablespoon olive oil. Coat with bread crumbs.
3. In a bowl, mix cheese, eggs and olives. Spread evenly in the prepared pan. Bake for 1 $1/4$ hours. Cool to room temperature.
4. For the sauce, combine tomatoes, 3 tablespoons olive oil, vinegar and capers.
5. Invert the baked torte onto a plate. Cut into wedges and top with sauce. Serve with greens, if desired. Makes 6-8 servings.

Brands may vary by region; substitute a similar product.

Side Dishes

LINDSAY
Spicy Pinto Beans with Olives

2 garlic cloves, minced
2 teaspoons olive oil
2 16-ounce cans pinto beans, rinsed and drained
1/2 cup chunky salsa
1 teaspoon ground cumin
1 6-ounce can Lindsay* Pitted Ripe Olives
1/4 cup shredded Monterey Jack or Mexican-blend cheese
2 tablespoons chopped cilantro

1. Cook garlic in oil in a medium saucepan over medium heat for 1 minute. Add beans, salsa and cumin; cook for 3 minutes, or until heated through.
2. Drain olives; cut crosswise in halves and stir into bean mixture. Simmer for 2 minutes, or until heated through.
3. Transfer to a serving dish; top with cheese and cilantro. Makes 6 servings.

Brands may vary by region; substitute a similar product.

MONTEREY MUSHROOMS
Rosemary Chicken and Mushroom Kabobs

1 garlic clove, minced
2 tablespoons olive oil
2 tablespoons finely chopped onion
3 tablespoons finely chopped rosemary
2 whole boneless, skinless chicken breasts, cut in 1/2-inch strips
12 large Monterey* Clean N Ready White Mushrooms
12 cherry tomatoes
12 asparagus spears, cut in half
6 metal kabob skewers

1. Combine garlic, olive oil, onion and rosemary in a bowl. Stir in chicken strips and marinate for 1 hour.
2. Preheat grill.
3. Remove chicken from the marinade and save the juices. Thread chicken strips, mushrooms, tomatoes and asparagus onto the skewers.
4. Place skewers on the top rack of the grill; cook, brushing occasionally with the reserved marinade, for 10-15 minutes, or until the chicken is cooked. Makes 4-6 servings.

Brands may vary by region; substitute a similar product.

HANNAH INTERNATIONAL
Bruschetta Italiano ▼

1 pound ziti
1/2 teaspoon salt
1 39-ounce jar Hannah* Bruschetta
1/2 cup grated Parmesan cheese

1. Boil ziti in salted water until al dente; drain pasta and place in a bowl.

2. Open Bruschetta and pour over warm pasta, stirring to blend.

3. Sprinkle with Parmesan. Makes 4-6 servings.

Tip: Use Bruschetta to spice up pizza, pasta, burgers, chicken or fish.

* Brands may vary by region; substitute a similar product.

Side Dishes

WALLACE FARMS, SKAGIT VALLEY'S BEST PRODUCE AND VALLEY PRIDE
Pacific Rim Potato and Veggie Stew ▲

12-14 small Washington
   red potatoes
   (2-2 $1/2$ pounds), halved

1 14-ounce can chicken broth

1 14-ounce can coconut milk
   (unsweetened)

2-inch piece ginger, with skin, cut
   in $1/4$-inch slices

1 teaspoon Thai yellow
   curry paste, optional

$1/4$ teaspoon red pepper flakes

1 stalk lemongrass,
   split and cut in 2-inch pieces

1 small red onion,
   cut in $1/4$-inch strips

1 tablespoon chopped garlic

2 tablespoons cornstarch

2 tablespoons soy sauce

1 cup $1/4$-inch-sliced celery

1 cup $1/4$-inch-sliced carrots

1 red bell pepper, diced

1 $1/2$ cups sugar snap or
   snow peas

Garnishes: chopped cilantro, sliced
   green onions, lime wedges,
   soy sauce, Asian hot sauce

1. In a large pot, combine the first 9 ingredients. Bring to a simmer, cover tightly, and simmer until potatoes are three-quarters done, about 10 minutes.

2. Whisk cornstarch into soy sauce and stir into the stew. Add celery, carrots and bell pepper. Return to a simmer, cover and cook until vegetables are almost tender, 5-6 minutes, adding peas during the last 2 minutes.

3. Sprinkle with cilantro and green onions. Pass remaining garnishes. Makes 6-8 servings.

Kathy Casey Food Studios.

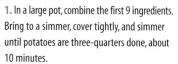

Chef and culinary diva Kathy Casey is the owner of Kathy Casey Food Studios and Dish D'Lish at the Pike Place Market. Casey pens the monthly column "Dishing" for the Seattle Times *and is the author of* Dishing with Kathy Casey. *For more information, visit www.KathyCasey.com.*

HANSEN'S BEVERAGE
Thai-Style Couscous ▲

1 can Hansen's* Mandarin Lime Soda

1 14 $1/2$-ounce can diced tomatoes, undrained

$1/2$ teaspoon red pepper flakes

$1/2$ teaspoon dried mint flakes

1 large garlic clove, crushed

10 ounces quick-cooking couscous

1 tablespoon toasted sesame oil

1 tablespoon lime juice

1 tablespoon soy sauce

2 green onions, minced

$1/2$ cup cilantro, snipped

1. Combine soda, diced tomatoes, red pepper flakes, mint and garlic in a large saucepan. Bring to a boil, remove from heat and stir in couscous. Cover and let stand 10 minutes.

2. In a small bowl, combine sesame oil, lime juice, soy sauce, green onions and cilantro; set aside.

3. Uncover couscous, fluff with a fork and stir in contents of the bowl. Makes 4-6 servings.

* Brands may vary by region; substitute a similar product.

Hansen's Natural

PREMIO
Sausage Stuffing ▼

6 links Premio* Mild Italian Sausage, casing removed
2 medium onions, chopped
2 stalks celery, diced or chopped
1 16-ounce package stuffing mix
2 cups chicken broth or hot water

1. In a large skillet, sauté sausage, onions and celery, breaking up sausage with a fork as it cooks.

2. When sausage is done, add stuffing mix and enough of the chicken broth for the desired consistency. (Do not pour off drippings.) Blend thoroughly.

3. Stuff bird loosely and follow cooking instructions for the bird. Makes enough to stuff a 14- to 16-pound bird.

Brands may vary by region; substitute a similar product.

Side Dishes ▮

MANN'S
Stringless Sugar Snap Pea Jubilee ▲

2 cups Mann's* Stringless Sugar Snap Peas
$^{1}/_{2}$ cup peeled orange slices
$^{1}/_{2}$ cup sliced strawberries
$^{1}/_{4}$ cup poppy seed dressing, your favorite brand
$^{1}/_{4}$ cup slivered almonds

1. Bring 2 quarts of water to a boil. Plunge sugar snap peas into boiling water; cook for 45 seconds. Drain and immediately plunge into ice water for 2 minutes. Drain.
2. Place snap peas in a bowl. Add orange slices and strawberries.
3. Add poppy seed dressing and toss gently. Sprinkle almonds on top. Makes 4 servings.

Tip: This dish is perfect for bridal or baby showers, Easter or Mother's Day brunch, or a barbecue.

Brands may vary by region; substitute a similar product.

GRIMMWAY FARMS
Roasted Carrots ▲

2 pounds Grimmway Farms* baby carrots
$^{1}/_{4}$ cup olive oil
1 $^{1}/_{4}$ teaspoons salt
$^{1}/_{2}$ teaspoon freshly ground black pepper
2 tablespoons minced fresh dill or parsley

1. Preheat oven to 400°F.
2. Toss carrots in a bowl with olive oil, salt and pepper. Transfer to a sheet pan in 1 layer and roast for 30 minutes, or until browned and tender.
3. Toss carrots with minced dill or parsley. Makes 6-8 servings.

Brands may vary by region; substitute a similar product.

WEST COAST VEGETABLE/ BLAND FARMS
Whole Sweet Onions with Sweet Pea Dressing

4 medium to large Bland Farms/West Coast Vegetable*
   Vidalia or Panoche sweet onions, peeled and cored
1 10-ounce box frozen sweet peas
¹/₂-1 cup sour cream
¹/₂-1 teaspoon sugar
Fresh herbs for garnish

1. Drop onions into boiling water for 5 minutes, or until as tender as desired. Lift onions from water and arrange on a platter.
2. Drop peas into the same water and cook until brightly colored and as tender as desired. Drain well.
3. In a bowl, mix sour cream with sugar to taste. Gently fold in peas.
4. Fill onions with sweet pea dressing and garnish with fresh herbs of your choice. Makes 4 servings.

Brands may vary by region; substitute a similar product.

WILSONBATIZ
Tomato Gratin

6 tablespoons olive oil
2 onions, sliced
2 red or green bell peppers, seeded and sliced into rounds
2 eggplants, thinly sliced
1 garlic clove, crushed
Salt and freshly ground pepper
2 pounds small zucchini, sliced into rounds
2 pounds WilsonBatiz* tomatoes, sliced
4 pinches of dried savory and thyme, mixed
¹/₂ cup freshly grated Parmesan cheese or fine bread crumbs
   (or mixture of both)

1. Preheat oven to 350°F. Heat 3 tablespoons olive oil in a large frying pan over medium heat. Add onions and brown slightly. Add peppers, eggplant, garlic, and salt and pepper to taste; cook gently, stirring occasionally, until softened.
2. Place the cooked vegetables in a 9-by-13-inch baking dish. Arrange zucchini and tomato slices on top in overlapping rows. Sprinkle with savory and thyme, salt and pepper to taste, and 2 tablespoons olive oil. Bake for 30 minutes.
3. Sprinkle with Parmesan and remaining olive oil. Bake for 15 minutes. Makes 6 servings.

Brands may vary by region; substitute a similar product.

❋WILSONBATIZ.

Entrées

TYSON
Beef Tenderloin Steaks with Blue Cheese Topping ◀

2 tablespoons cream cheese, softened
4 teaspoons crumbled blue cheese
4 teaspoons plain yogurt
2 teaspoons minced onion
Dash of ground white pepper
4 Tyson* beef tenderloin steaks, cut 1 inch thick (about 1 pound)
1 large garlic clove, halved
1/2 teaspoon salt
2 teaspoons chopped fresh parsley

1. Preheat broiler.
2. Combine cream cheese, blue cheese, yogurt, minced onion and white pepper in a small bowl. Set aside. Rub steaks with garlic. Wash hands.
3. Place steaks on a rack in a broiler pan so the surface of the beef is 2-3 inches from the heat. Broil, turning once, 13-15 minutes for medium-rare to medium (internal temperature 150°F to 160°F). About 1-2 minutes before steaks are done, spoon cheese mixture evenly over steaks. Broil until cheese is bubbling.
Serving suggestion: Season with salt and sprinkle with parsley. Serve with a crisp green salad and crusty bread. Refrigerate leftovers. Makes 4 servings.

Brands may vary by region; substitute a similar product.

MARIANI
Black Magic Beef Steaks with Balsamic Dried Plum Sauce ▲

4 beef tenderloin steaks, cut 1 inch thick
1 teaspoon coarsely ground black pepper
1 cup (about 6 ounces) coarsely chopped Mariani/Kirkland Signature dried plums
2/3 cup beef broth, divided
1/2 cup finely chopped green onions, white part only
1/3 cup balsamic vinegar
1 teaspoon cornstarch
1/4 cup finely chopped green onion tops

1. Season steaks with pepper. Grill, uncovered, over medium (ash-covered) coals 13-15 minutes for medium-rare to medium, turning occasionally.
2. In a medium saucepan, combine dried plums, 1/3 cup beef broth, green onions (white part) and vinegar. Bring to a boil, reduce heat and simmer for 5 minutes.
3. In a small bowl, combine remaining beef broth and cornstarch, stirring to dissolve; stir into the sauce. Cook until thickened and bubbly, stirring occasionally.
4. Place the steaks on a serving platter. Spoon the sauce over the steaks; sprinkle with green onion tops. Makes 4 servings.

EXCEL BEEF
Bistro-Style New York Strip Steaks ▲

2 teaspoons chopped fresh rosemary
2 teaspoons chopped fresh thyme
2 teaspoons salt
2 teaspoons pepper
4 Excel Beef* 10-ounce New York strip steaks
4 ounces shallots
4 ounces prepared demi-glace
16 ounces frites (French fries)
4 ounces salad greens
2 tablespoons prepared vinaigrette

1. Combine rosemary, thyme, salt and pepper. Sprinkle half of herb mixture on steaks; reserve remaining mixture.

2. Grill or sauté steaks until cooked to desired doneness.

3. For sautéed steaks, slice shallots and cook in the pan drippings until golden brown and soft. Stir in demi-glace, bring to a simmer and adjust seasoning. For grilled steaks, cut shallots in thicker slices and grill. Place demi-glace in a saucepan, bring to a simmer and stir in grilled shallots.

4. To make frites, deep-fry potato strips in 360°F oil until golden brown. Toss with the reserved herb mixture.

5. Place salad greens in a bowl and toss with vinaigrette.

6. Top each steak with sauce and seasoned frites. Serve with salad. Makes 4 servings.

* Brands may vary by region; substitute a similar product.

EXCEL

EMMBER CLASSIC
Sliced Roast Beef Tex-Mex
Fajita Skillet ▲

3/4 cup prepared fajita sauce
3 ounces sliced mushrooms, grilled
3 ounces sliced onion, grilled
20 ounces Emmber Classic* Sliced Roast Beef Top Round
2 ounces deep-fried tortilla strips
1 cup diced avocado
4 teaspoons chopped cilantro

1. Combine fajita sauce, mushrooms and onions in a bowl.

2. Cut sliced roast beef into 1-inch strips. Heat on a flat grill until warm.

3. Heat a cast-iron skillet until smoking. Place the vegetable mixture in the skillet, top with roast beef, and garnish with crispy tortilla strips, avocado and cilantro. Serve immediately. Makes 4 servings.

* Brands may vary by region; substitute a similar product.

SWIFT
Grilled Strip Steaks with
Tomato-Pesto Glaze ▼

6 Swift Premium Beef Top Loin (New York) Steaks, 1 inch thick
$1/4$ cup butter, softened
2 tablespoons coarsely chopped oil-packed sun-dried tomatoes
2 tablespoons prepared basil pesto
Salt and pepper

1. Place steaks on a grid over medium, ash-covered coals. Grill, uncovered, for 15-18 minutes for medium-rare to medium doneness, turning once.

2. Meanwhile, place butter, sun-dried tomatoes and pesto in a food processor or blender. Cover and process until almost smooth.

3. Remove steaks from the grill; season to taste with salt and pepper. Spread the glaze over the hot steaks. Makes 6 servings.

Swift tip: To broil, place steaks on a rack in a broiler pan so the surface of the beef is 3-4 inches from the heat. Broil 13-17 minutes for medium-rare to medium doneness, turning once.

Swift & Company

BRAWLEY BEEF
Bacon-Wrapped Tenderloin

1 choice Brawley Beef* tenderloin
1 tablespoon vegetable oil
2 tablespoons whole-grain mustard
2 tablespoons chopped shallots
1 tablespoon chopped garlic
1 tablespoon chopped fresh thyme
Kosher salt
Freshly ground black pepper
15 thick slices bacon

1. Preheat oven to 350°F.

2. Clean tenderloin by removing all silver skin. Combine oil and mustard and spread evenly over tenderloin. Stir together shallots, garlic and thyme in a small bowl; rub onto tenderloin. Season to taste with salt and pepper. Wrap bacon around tenderloin and tie with butcher's twine.

3. Sear the roast in a large pan over medium heat, turning often to ensure even browning. After the bacon has been rendered, place the meat on a rack and roast for 15-20 minutes, or until the internal temperature is 130°F.

4. Remove roast from the oven and let rest for 5-10 minutes. Remove string, slice meat and serve. Makes 6 servings.

This recipe was created at the Park Hyatt Carmel, Highlands Inn.
* Brands may vary by region; substitute a similar product.

AUSTRALIAN LAMB
Honey and Garlic Lamb Rack
with Orzo Salad ▲

2 Frenched racks of Australian lamb

MARINADE
1 1/2 cups red wine
2 tablespoons honey
3 garlic cloves, crushed
1 tablespoon fresh thyme leaves

ORZO SALAD
1 pound orzo pasta

Juice and grated peel of 1 lemon
2 tablespoons extra-virgin olive oil
1/4 cup chopped black olives
Kernels cut from 2 ears fresh corn
1/4 cup chopped cilantro
1/4 cup chopped parsley
Salt and freshly ground pepper
to taste

1. Make 4 shallow slashes, about 1/2 inch deep, down the meat side of each rack. Combine the marinade ingredients and mix well. Pour marinade into a large, flat glass or ceramic dish. Add the lamb, turning to coat all sides and brushing into the slashes. Marinate, meat side down, for 2-3 hours or overnight in the refrigerator.

2. To make orzo salad, cook pasta according to package directions and drain well. Let cool slightly, then transfer to a large bowl and add the remaining ingredients. Toss well and season to taste.

3. Take the meat from the marinade and pat dry. Place the marinade in a small pan and bring to a boil. Reduce heat and simmer until liquid is starting to thicken to a glaze. Keep warm.

4. Heat a barbecue or grill to medium-high and cook the lamb until internal temperature is 135-140°F (about 10-12 minutes each side). Let rest for 5 minutes.

5. Spoon orzo salad onto a large platter and place the whole racks on top; or separate the lamb into chops and serve on individual plates. Spoon the glaze over the chops and serve with a green salad. Makes 4-6 servings.

Tip: Salad can be made 2-3 hours ahead and served cold with the lamb.

THE
AUSTRALIAN LAMB
COMPANY INC.

Entrées I

AUSTRALIAN LAMB
Barbecued Lamb Leg with Grilled Vegetables and Pesto Dressing ▼

1 whole boneless leg of Australian lamb, butterflied* and trimmed

MARINADE
1 cup red wine
1/4 cup olive oil
2 garlic cloves, crushed
2 teaspoons dried oregano
2 teaspoons dried basil
Freshly ground black pepper

GRILLED VEGETABLES
Halved red bell peppers, sliced
  eggplant and zucchini,
  portobello mushrooms
  and asparagus
Olive oil

PESTO DRESSING
1/3 cup dry-roasted or
  blanched almonds
1 cup chopped Italian parsley
1/2 cup chopped fresh basil
1/4 cup extra-virgin olive oil
1 tablespoon lemon juice
2 tablespoons soft goat or
  feta cheese

1. Place lamb in a shallow ceramic or glass casserole dish. Combine the marinade ingredients and pour over the lamb. Cover and refrigerate for 2-3 hours or overnight, turning over once or twice during that time. Discard marinade.

2. Preheat a hooded barbecue to medium-high. Place the lamb on the grill and sear on all sides for 1-2 minutes to brown. Reduce heat to medium, pull down the hood and cook lamb, turning once or twice, about 10-15 minutes on each side, or until internal temperature is 135-140°F in the thickest part of the leg. Remove from the grill and transfer to a plate. Cover loosely with foil and let rest for 10 minutes before slicing.

3. While the lamb is resting, brush the vegetables with oil and grill until lightly browned and tender. Arrange on a large platter with the sliced lamb.

4. To make the pesto dressing, place almonds, parsley, basil, oil and lemon juice in a food processor and process to a coarse paste. Add cheese and process just to combine. Makes 6-8 servings.

* To butterfly the lamb, remove netting and open out the leg to make as flat as possible. With a meat mallet or rolling pin, gently pound to an even, desired thickness.

THE
AUSTRALIAN LAMB
COMPANY INC.

AUSTRALIAN LAMB
Herb-Crusted Lamb Loin Chops with Tomato Mint Salad ▲

8 Australian lamb loin chops

1-2 tablespoons Dijon or
   coarse-grain mustard

Olive oil

Lemon wedges

HERB CRUST

1/2 cup fresh bread crumbs or
   diced baguette

4 large leaves fresh basil

1 tablespoon grated
   Parmesan cheese

1 tablespoon pine nuts, optional

TOMATO MINT SALAD

1 pint cherry tomatoes, halved

8-10 pitted green olives, sliced

1/4 cup sliced fresh mint leaves

1 tablespoon wine vinegar

Salt and freshly ground pepper
   to taste

1. Place the crust ingredients in a small blender (or coffee grinder in small batches) and process to combine. Cover the chops with Dijon mustard. Tip crust ingredients onto a plate and press chops firmly onto mixture to coat both sides. Cover with plastic and refrigerate for 10 minutes to set crust.

2. Combine salad ingredients and set aside.

3. Heat a nonstick or cast-iron pan to medium and add enough oil to coat. Add chops and cook for 3-4 minutes on each side, or until cooked as desired (suggested internal temperature of 145°F) and the crust is crisp and browned. Serve with the salad and lemon wedges. A green salad and the rest of the baguette are the perfect match for this dish. Makes 4 servings.

THE
AUSTRALIAN LAMB
COMPANY INC.

Entrées ∎

PLUME DE VEAU
Veal and Peppers

1 large red bell pepper, seeded and sliced
1 large green bell pepper, seeded and sliced
1 onion, minced
1 tablespoon minced garlic
1 5 ¹/₂-ounce can low-sodium V8 juice
¹/₄ cup red wine
Pinch of dried thyme
Pinch of red pepper flakes
Pinch of Italian seasoning
Salt and pepper to taste
1 pound Plume De Veau* veal cut for stew

1. In a soup pot, combine bell peppers, onion, garlic, V8, wine and seasonings. Place veal on top.
2. Bring to a boil, reduce heat, cover and simmer for 7 hours, or until veal is tender. Makes 4 servings.

Brands may vary by region; substitute a similar product.

PLUME DE VEAU
Veal Marsala

2 tablespoons butter
2 tablespoons olive oil
1-1 ¹/₂ pounds Plume De Veau* veal scaloppine
All-purpose flour
Salt and pepper
Dash of ground ginger
¹/₂ cup Marsala wine
¹/₄ cup chicken broth
3 tablespoons chopped fresh parsley

1. Heat butter and oil in a skillet over medium heat. Dredge veal in flour and brown quickly in the skillet. Season to taste with salt, pepper and ground ginger.
2. Pour Marsala over veal and continue cooking until wine is reduced by half. Turn scaloppine once during this time. When the wine is reduced and the meat is tender, remove the scaloppine to a hot platter.
3. Add chicken broth to the pan. Bring to a boil and add parsley. Pour juices over the meat. Makes 4 servings.

Brands may vary by region; substitute a similar product.

Easy Cooking The Costco Way

PLUME DE VEAU
Grilled Veal Chops with Tarragon

4 Plume De Veau* veal loin or rib chops, cut 3/4 inch thick
1/2 cup chicken broth
3 teaspoons chopped fresh tarragon, divided
1 teaspoon kosher salt
1/4 teaspoon pepper

1. Place veal chops in a shallow dish with the chicken broth. Cover and refrigerate for 30 minutes. Drain chops, discarding broth.
2. Preheat grill to medium. Combine 1 1/2 teaspoons of the tarragon, salt and pepper. Rub veal with the tarragon mixture.
3. Grill chops, turning once, for 10-12 minutes, or until cooked to taste. Serve chops garnished with the remaining 1 1/2 teaspoons tarragon. Makes 4 servings.

* Brands may vary by region; substitute a similar product.

RICHMOND NEW ZEALAND FARM FRESH
Beef Disks

1 pound Kirkland Signature ground beef
1 teaspoon salt
3 tablespoons water

1. Place all ingredients in a food processor and chop until a coarse, sticky paste forms, about 1 minute.
2. Spread the mixture on a sheet of plastic wrap and shape into a cylinder 1 1/2 inches in diameter. Twist ends of plastic wrap to seal. Freeze for about 10 minutes.
3. Unwrap and carefully slice into 1/2-inch disks; immediately sear in a hot oiled frying pan. Remove to a plate.
4. The disks will now be quite resilient. You can add them to any kind of simmer sauce—they make an excellent curry. Heat for 5 minutes in the sauce and serve over rice. Or brush with your favorite glaze and cook for 1 minute on the grill. Makes about 20 disks.

RICHMOND.
NEW ZEALAND FARM FRESH

Entrées I

TYSON
Pork Roast Tangerine

1 tablespoon dry mustard
1 teaspoon salt
¹/₄ teaspoon pepper
1 Tyson Fresh Boneless Pork Loin Roast, about 3 pounds
1 tangerine or orange
1 cup tangerine juice or orange juice
¹/₄ cup honey
1 tablespoon cornstarch
2 tablespoons butter

1. Preheat oven to 325°F.
2. Combine mustard, salt and pepper in a small bowl. Rub roast with the mixture. Place roast on a rack in a shallow roasting pan; insert a meat thermometer in the thickest part. Wash hands. Roast pork for 1-1 ¹/₂ hours, or until done (internal temperature 155°F).
3. Meanwhile, rinse tangerine; remove and reserve peel. Section tangerine; set aside. Remove white membrane from peel and cut about 2 tablespoons julienne strips. Combine julienned peel and 1 cup water in a small saucepan. Bring to a boil; reduce heat and simmer for about 15 minutes. Drain.
4. Combine tangerine juice and honey in a small saucepan. Mix together cornstarch and 1 tablespoon water, and stir into juice-honey mixture. Cook over medium heat until thickened and bubbly, stirring constantly. Add butter and cooked peel; cook until butter melts, stirring constantly.
Serving suggestion: Slice the pork roast and arrange on a serving platter. Garnish with tangerine sections and spoon sauce over all. Serve with sour cream mashed potatoes and glazed baby carrots. Refrigerate leftovers. Makes 12 servings.

CLASSICO
Pork Medallions Arrabbiata ▲

8 ounces penne rigate pasta
2 tablespoons olive oil
1 onion, cut in wedges
1/2 green bell pepper, cut in strips
1/2 red bell pepper, cut in strips
1 pound pork tenderloin, cut in 1/2-inch slices
2 garlic cloves, finely chopped
1 32-ounce jar Classico* Tomato Basil Pasta Sauce
1/4 teaspoon dried thyme
1 teaspoon red pepper flakes

1. Cook pasta according to package directions; drain. Set aside and keep warm.
2. Heat olive oil in a skillet over medium heat. Cook onion and bell peppers until tender, stirring frequently. Remove vegetables from the skillet and set aside.
3. Add pork and garlic to the pan. Cook until the pork is browned on both sides. Add pasta sauce, thyme and red pepper flakes. Bring to a simmer. Simmer for 10 minutes, or until the pork is tender, stirring occasionally.
4. Add the vegetables. Cook until heated through. Serve with the hot pasta. Makes 8 servings.

Brands may vary by region; substitute a similar product.

HEINZ
Hot and Sweet Barbecue Sauce ▲

1 1/3 cups Heinz Tomato Ketchup
1/4 cup Heinz* Apple Cider Vinegar
2 tablespoons Heinz* 57 Sauce or Worcestershire Sauce
1 10- to 12-ounce jar orange marmalade
1-2 teaspoons chili powder

1. Combine all ingredients in a small saucepan and mix well. Cook over low heat until heated through and blended.
2. Brush the sauce on chicken, pork or beef during the last 5-10 minutes of grilling time. Bring any remaining sauce to a boil to serve with the meat. Makes 2 2/3 cups.

Brands may vary by region; substitute a similar product.

PREMIO
Italian Sausage with Fusilli, White Beans and Escarole ▼

1/4 cup olive oil

1 1/2 cups onions cut in 1/2-inch dice

10 garlic cloves, thinly sliced

2 bay leaves

1 large head escarole, trimmed of tough parts, washed and torn in 2-inch squares

2 cups chicken broth

8 links Premio* Mild Italian Sausage, cooked according to package directions and quartered

1 1/2 cups cooked cannellini beans

Salt and freshly ground black pepper

1 pound fusilli, cooked until al dente and drained

3/4 cup grated Romano cheese

1. Heat oil in a large heavy-bottomed sauce pot. Add onions and sauté until soft, 5-8 minutes. Add garlic and cook gently for 2-3 minutes. Add bay leaves.

2. Raise heat to high. Add escarole and stir until wilted. Stir in chicken broth and cook, uncovered, until reduced by a third. Add sausage and beans; season to taste with salt and pepper.

3. Simmer for 15-20 minutes, loosely covered. Combine with cooked pasta. Serve with grated cheese and ground black pepper. Makes 6-8 servings.

Brands may vary by region; substitute a similar product.

KIRKLAND SIGNATURE/CARANDO
Spiral-Sliced Ham with Warm Maple-Apple Salsa

1 Kirkland Signature/Carando* Hickory-Smoked Spiral-Sliced Ham
$1/2$ cup butter
4 medium cooking apples, cored and chopped
1 cup walnut pieces, toasted
$1/2$ cup pure maple syrup

1. Heat ham according to package directions.
2. Melt butter in a large skillet. Add apples and stir-fry over high heat until tender-crisp. Stir in walnuts and syrup; heat through. Ladle over ham slices to serve. Makes about 10 servings.

Brands may vary by region; substitute a similar product.

PRAIRIEFRESH
Pork Roast with Applesauce Salsa

APPLESAUCE SALSA
2 cups applesauce
1 cup tomato-based hot salsa
2 Granny Smith apples, chopped
1 tablespoon cider vinegar
1 tablespoon ground cinnamon
$1/2$ teaspoon ground cloves
$1/2$ cup raisins

3- to 4-pound Natural PrairieFresh Premium Boneless Pork Loin
2 tablespoons brown sugar
2 tablespoons red wine vinegar
1 teaspoon ground nutmeg
$1/4$ teaspoon salt

1. Combine the salsa ingredients and blend well. Refrigerate overnight.
2. Preheat oven to 350°F. Score the top of the pork loin and place in a shallow pan.
3. Mix brown sugar, vinegar, nutmeg and salt. Rub mixture over pork loin.
4. Roast for 1 $1/2$ hours, or until internal temperature is 160°F. Let loin rest for 10 minutes before slicing. Serve with Applesauce Salsa.
Makes 6-8 servings.

PRAIRIEFRESH
PREMIUM PORK

SWIFT
Chinese Sesame Pork Back Ribs

3 slabs Swift Natural Pork Back Ribs (about 7 pounds)
Salt and pepper
2 7- to 8-ounce jars hoisin sauce
1/3 cup packed brown sugar
1/3 cup fresh lemon juice
2 tablespoons minced fresh ginger
1 1/2 tablespoons toasted sesame oil
1 tablespoon minced garlic
Chopped cilantro, optional
Toasted sesame seeds, optional

1. Remove the thin, papery membrane from the back side of each pork back-rib rack. Slide the tip of a small knife under at the third rib and loosen until you can peel the thin sheet off. Cut each rack in half crosswise. Season to taste with salt and pepper.

2. Combine hoisin sauce, brown sugar, lemon juice, ginger, sesame oil and garlic in a small bowl; reserve.

3. Prepare grill for indirect grilling. Place ribs on a grid over a drip pan (or over unused burners for gas grills). Grill, covered, for 1 1/2 hours, or until tender, brushing with the reserved sauce during the last 5-10 minutes. Garnish with cilantro and sesame seeds. Makes 6 servings.

Swift tip: Preheat oven to 325°F. Place seasoned ribs in 1 large or 2 small roasting pans; cover tightly. Roast for 1 1/4-1 1/2 hours, or until fork tender. Remove ribs from oven. Increase oven temperature to 375°F. Pour off drippings. Brush ribs with sauce; return to oven and cook until glazed, about 10-15 minutes.

Swift.
Swift & Company®

SMITHFIELD
Pork Tenderloin Medallions with
Raspberry Sauce ▲

1 Smithfield* whole pork
    tenderloin, about 1 pound,
    cut in 8 crosswise pieces

Cayenne pepper

2 teaspoons butter

5 tablespoons
    red raspberry preserves

2 tablespoons red wine vinegar

1/2 teaspoon prepared horseradish

1 garlic clove, minced

1 tablespoon ketchup

1/2 teaspoon soy sauce

2 kiwi fruit, peeled and thinly sliced

1/2 pint fresh raspberries

1. With heel of hand, gently press each pork medallion to 1-inch thickness; lightly sprinkle both sides with cayenne to taste. Heat butter in a nonstick skillet over medium-high heat; add pork medallions and cook for 3-4 minutes on each side.

2. Meanwhile, in a small saucepan stir together preserves, vinegar, horseradish, garlic, ketchup and soy sauce; simmer over low heat for 2 minutes, stirring occasionally; keep warm.

3. Place medallions on a serving plate. Spoon sauce over medallions and top with some kiwi slices. Garnish serving plate with remaining kiwi slices and raspberries. Makes 4 servings.

Brands may vary by region; substitute a similar product.

Smithfield.

Entrées I

REYNOLDS
Apple-Stuffed Pork Chops ▼

Reynolds Wrap Heavy Duty Aluminum Foil
1 6-ounce package stuffing mix for pork
¹/₂ cup chopped apple
¹/₄ cup sweetened dried cranberries
4 boneless center-cut pork chops, 1 ¹/₄ inches thick
¹/₂ teaspoon seasoned salt
¹/₄ teaspoon pepper
2 tablespoons packed brown sugar
1 tablespoon butter, melted

1. Preheat oven to 425°F. Line a 10-by-15-by-1-inch pan with foil.
2. Prepare stuffing mix according to package directions. Stir in apple and cranberries.
3. Cut a pocket in each pork chop with a sharp knife. Place chops in the foil-lined pan; season with salt and pepper. Stuff each chop with ¹/₂ cup of stuffing; press to flatten.
4. Bake for 18-20 minutes; remove from oven. Preheat broiler. Mix brown sugar and melted butter; brush onto chops. Broil 3-4 inches from the heat for 5-8 minutes, or until browned. Makes 4 servings.

KRAFT
BBQ Pork Chops and Stuffing Dinner ▲

1 small onion, sliced
1 small green bell pepper, sliced
2 tablespoons oil, divided
4 bone-in or boneless pork chops, 1/2 inch thick
1 6-ounce package Stove Top* Stuffing Mix for Pork
3/4 cup Kraft* Thick 'N Spicy or Bull's-Eye* Original Barbecue Sauce

1. Cook onion and pepper in 1 tablespoon oil in a medium skillet on medium-high heat until tender-crisp; remove from skillet.
2. Add remaining oil and chops to the skillet. Cook for 8-10 minutes, or until cooked through. Meanwhile, prepare stuffing according to package directions.
3. Spoon onion mixture over chops. Top with barbecue sauce; cover. Reduce heat to low and cook until sauce is thoroughly heated. Serve with stuffing. Makes 4 servings.

Kraft Kitchens tip: Substitute Stove Top Cornbread Stuffing for Stuffing Mix for Pork.

Brands may vary by region; substitute a similar product.

KRAFT
Quick Chicken and Asparagus Risotto ▲

1 pound boneless, skinless chicken breast halves
1 tablespoon oil
1 10 3/4-ounce can condensed cream of chicken soup
1 1/3 cups milk
2 cups Minute White Rice, uncooked
1 pound thin asparagus spears, cut in 2-inch pieces
Kraft 100% Grated Parmesan Cheese

1. Cook chicken in oil in a large skillet on medium heat for 3 minutes a side, or until cooked through. Remove from skillet and set aside.
2. Add soup and milk to the skillet; bring to a boil.
3. Stir in rice and asparagus. Top with chicken; cover. Cook on low heat for 5 minutes. Sprinkle with Parmesan before serving. Makes 4 servings.

Kraft Kitchens tip: Asparagus spears should be bright green and free of blemishes. Choose stalks that are straight, uniformly sized (either all thick or all thin) and firm.

Chicken
The Costco Way

One of Costco's most popular food items is its succulent rotisserie chicken, roasted fresh daily in the warehouses. Costco member Rhonda Barranco of Kahului, Hawaii, has perfected the art of using this exceptional chicken in a variety of recipes. For more Costco rotisserie chicken recipes, see her Web site, www.rhondas-recipes.com.

The versatile rotisserie chicken

Sesame Chicken Salad

1 cup mayonnaise
1 tablespoon Asian sesame oil
1 tablespoon sugar or Splenda
$1/8$ teaspoon ground ginger, or 2 tablespoons minced fresh ginger
2 cups cubed breast meat from Kirkland Signature rotisserie chicken
$1/2$ small head Napa cabbage, thinly sliced
2 green onions, chopped
1 tablespoon sesame seeds, toasted
1 large carrot, shredded

1. Combine mayonnaise, sesame oil, sugar and ginger. Cover and refrigerate for several hours.
2. Place cabbage, carrots and green onion in a large bowl, and toss. Sprinkle the chicken and sesame seeds on top of the salad. Serve with the dressing right away. Makes 4 servings.
Tip: Sprinkle the salad with fried noodles for added crunch.

Curry Chicken Quiche

CRUST
$1/2$ cup chopped onions
$1/4$ cup butter
2 $1/2$ cups crushed saltine crackers (1 package)
$1/2$ cup olive oil
1 tablespoon curry powder

FILLING
3-4 eggs
1 $1/2$ cups cream or half-and-half
2 cups shredded Monterey Jack and Cheddar cheese
2 cups cubed Kirkland Signature rotisserie chicken
1-2 teaspoons curry powder

1. Preheat oven to 350°F.
2. To make the crust, crumble crackers in an 8 $1/2$-by-10-inch glass baking dish. Sauté onions in butter until softened. Add crackers, onion and curry mixing to the olive oil and toss gently .
3. Line the baking dish with cracker mix. Try to get the mix to stay on the sides.
4. To make the filling, beat eggs in a medium bowl. Add cream and combine well. Stir in cheese, chicken and curry powder to taste. Pour over the cracker crumbs.
5. Bake for 30 minutes, or longer to brown. Makes 4-6 servings.
Tip: This can also be made without a crust. Just coat the pan with cooking spray.

Southwestern Chicken Salad
with Chipotle Caesar Dressing

1 cup mayonnaise
1 tablespoon soy sauce
1 tablespoon brown sugar or Splenda
1 tablespoon chicken broth
2 teaspoons diced chipotle peppers in adobo sauce (or just the sauce)
1 tablespoon lemon or lime juice
1 large head romaine lettuce, torn in bite-size pieces
2 cups diced or shredded breast meat from Kirkland Signature rotisserie chicken
2 tomatoes, sliced
$1/2$ cup grated Parmesan cheese
1 small (7- to 8 $3/4$-ounce) can corn, drained
1 cup black beans, optional

1. Combine mayonnaise, soy sauce, brown sugar, chicken broth, chipotle peppers and lemon juice. Cover and refrigerate for up to 24 hours.
2. Place lettuce, chicken, tomatoes and cheese in a large bowl. Add dressing and toss.
3. Serve the corn and black beans in bowls on the table so you can add them to the salad as you like. Makes 4 servings.

Chicken Enchiladas Verde

12 corn tortillas
4 cups shredded Kirkland Signature rotisserie chicken
4 cups shredded Monterey Jack and Cheddar cheese
4 7-ounce cans green (tomatillo) enchilada sauce
Sour cream

1. Preheat oven to 350°F.
2. Put tortillas in a zipper-lock bag (do not zip) and warm for about 1 minute in the microwave.
3. In a large glass baking dish, fill each tortilla with chicken and cheese; pour about $1/4$ cup of green sauce over the filling and roll up. Pour remaining sauce over the enchiladas and sprinkle with cheese.
4. Bake for 20 minutes, or until bubbling. Add a dollop of sour cream to each serving. Makes 6 servings.
Tip: Garnish with cilantro for company!

GOLD KIST FARMS
Chicken Cakes with Chipotle Mayonnaise ◀

1 1/2 pounds Gold Kist Farms*
  boneless, skinless split
  chicken breasts
1/4 cup all-purpose flour
1 egg, lightly beaten
1/2 cup panko
2 tablespoons olive oil

CHIPOTLE MAYONNAISE
1 cup mayonnaise
1 tablespoon lime juice
2 teaspoons minced shallot
1 teaspoon minced garlic
1 teaspoon Chipotle
  Chile Pepper**
Salt

CHICKEN CAKES
1/2 cup panko (Japanese
  bread crumbs)
1/2 cup minced shallot
1 egg, lightly beaten
2 tablespoons jalapeño
  pepper jelly, melted, cooled
2 tablespoons minced
  fresh cilantro
Salt and pepper to taste

1. Place chicken in a single layer in a saucepan. Barely cover with water; bring to a boil. Reduce heat, cover and simmer for 12-15 minutes, or until chicken is no longer pink inside. Drain, cool and finely chop (about 3 cups).
2. Combine ingredients for Chipotle Mayonnaise in a small bowl. Reserve 6 tablespoons for preparing chicken cakes. Refrigerate remainder to serve with cakes.
3. Mix chicken cake ingredients, including the reserved chicken and Chipotle Mayonnaise. Divide into twelve 1/4-cup portions (or 1-2 rounded tablespoons per cake for appetizers).
4. Place flour, egg and panko in separate shallow dishes. Lightly coat both sides of each cake with flour, egg and then panko. Cover and refrigerate until ready to cook. The cakes can also be frozen at this point and then thawed in the refrigerator before frying.
5. Heat oil in a nonstick skillet until very hot but not smoking. Cook cakes, without crowding, until golden brown, about 3 minutes per side; drain. Serve with Chipotle Mayonnaise. Makes 6 entrée servings or 24-36 appetizers.

Brands may vary by region; substitute a similar product.
**Find Chipotle Chile Pepper in the spice section of a supermarket. Or substitute 1 teaspoon adobo sauce from canned chipotle chiles.*

BEE SWEET CITRUS
Chicken with Citrus Sauce ▲

4 chicken breast halves with skin
5 teaspoons ground cumin, divided
Salt and pepper
4 tablespoons olive oil, divided
3 garlic cloves, pressed
1/2 cup chicken broth
1/2 cup fresh Bee Sweet Citrus* orange juice
1/2 cup fresh Bee Sweet Citrus* lemon juice
2 teaspoons grated Bee Sweet Citrus orange peel
2 teaspoons grated Bee Sweet Citrus lemon peel
Bee Sweet Citrus fruit, sliced
1/2 cup fresh cilantro leaves

1. Preheat oven to 425°F.
2. Sprinkle each breast with 1 teaspoon cumin and salt and pepper to taste; rub seasoning into skin. Heat 2 tablespoons oil in an ovenproof skillet. Brown chicken, skin side down, over medium-high heat. Turn chicken and place skillet in oven. Bake for 20 minutes, or until cooked through.
3. Remove chicken to a plate. Add remaining oil to drippings in skillet. Add garlic and sauté briefly. Stir in broth, orange and lemon juice, orange and lemon peel, and remaining cumin. Cook to reduce to 1 cup.
4. Pour sauce over chicken. Garnish with sliced citrus fruit and cilantro. Makes 4 servings.

Brands may vary by region; substitute a similar product.

Entrées I

TARANTINO'S
Italian Stuffed Chicken ▼

6 boneless, skinless chicken breast halves
1 tablespoon chopped garlic
1/2 cup sliced mushrooms
1 tablespoon oil
1/4 cup Marsala wine
1/2 cup Italian seasoned bread crumbs
1/2 cup blanched chopped spinach, squeezed dry
3 green onions, sliced
1/4 cup chopped fresh basil
1 tablespoon grated Parmesan cheese
1/4 teaspoon salt
1/4 teaspoon pepper
8 ounces Tarantino's* mild Italian sausage, casings removed
1/4 cup seasoned flour
1/4 cup light olive oil

1. Preheat oven to 350°F. Slice into the side of each chicken breast to create a pocket.

2. Sauté garlic and mushrooms in 1 tablespoon oil. Add Marsala and simmer until mushrooms have absorbed the wine. Set aside to cool.

3. Add bread crumbs, spinach, green onions, basil, Parmesan, salt and pepper to the cooled mushrooms. Mix in sausage until everything is incorporated.

4. Open the chicken breast pockets and fill with the stuffing. Dredge in seasoned flour and sauté in olive oil over medium heat until lightly browned. Finish cooking in the oven for 15 minutes, or until chicken is firm to the touch and has an internal temperature of 160°F.

5. Serve with a Marsala sauce or tomato sauce. This is also good served without a sauce if you so desire. Makes 6 servings.

Recipe provided by Chef David Chenelle.
*Brands may vary by region; substitute a similar product.

AMERICA'S KITCHEN
Chicken Pot Pie with Tarragon Cream Sauce ▲

1 tablespoon butter
1 tablespoon flour
1 cup half-and-half
1 teaspoon dried tarragon or 2 teaspoons chopped fresh tarragon
1 chicken bouillon cube
3/4 teaspoon salt
1/8 teaspoon pepper
1 tablespoon sour cream
America's Kitchen Chicken Pot Pie, prepared according
    to package directions

1. Melt butter in a saucepan over low heat. Whisk in flour to make a roux.
2. Gradually add half-and-half, whisking thoroughly. Stir in tarragon, bouillon cube, salt and pepper. Cook until smooth. Remove from heat and whisk in sour cream.
3. Serve with chicken pot pie. Makes 6 servings.

MRS. DASH AND MOLLY McBUTTER
Chicken and Rice Dinner Bundles ▲

4 sheets (12 by 18 inches) heavy-duty aluminum foil
4 4-ounce boneless chicken breasts
1 1/3 cups instant rice
12 thin slices red onion, diced
12 thin slices red bell pepper, diced
1 small zucchini, cubed
4 teaspoons Molly McButter Natural Butter Sprinkles*
4 teaspoons Mrs. Dash Original Seasoning Blend*
1 1/3 cups low-sodium chicken broth

1. Preheat grill to medium-high.
2. Place foil sheets on a flat surface; turn up edges to form a lip. For each serving, place 1 chicken breast on a sheet of foil; arrange 1/3 cup rice around chicken. Top with 3 slices onion, 3 slices bell pepper and 1/4 of the zucchini. Sprinkle with 1 teaspoon Molly McButter.
3. Double-fold top and one end of foil. Stir Mrs. Dash into chicken broth and pour 1/3 cup into each package. Fold end tightly, leaving room for heat to circulate and rice to expand.
4. Place packets on the grill and cook for 12 minutes.
5. Open packets carefully and remove chicken to serving plates. Stir rice and vegetables together and place on plates with chicken. Makes 4 servings.

* Brands may vary by region; substitute a similar product.

TYSON
Chicken with Raspberry Sauce

4 Tyson Fresh Boneless, Skinless Chicken Breasts,
   or 4 Tyson Individually Fresh Frozen Boneless, Skinless Chicken
   Breasts without Rib Meat (see note)
1/2 teaspoon salt
1/4 teaspoon pepper
1 tablespoon butter
1/2 cup finely chopped onion
1/2 cup Tyson Chicken Broth
1/4 cup seedless raspberry jam
2 tablespoons raspberry vinegar

1. Sprinkle both sides of chicken with salt and pepper. Wash hands.
2. Melt butter in a large nonstick skillet over medium-high heat.
Add chicken and cook for 3 minutes per side, or until browned. Transfer
chicken to a plate; cover and keep warm.
3. Reduce heat to medium. Add onions to the skillet; cook, stirring, for
2-3 minutes, or until tender. Whisk in broth, jam and vinegar.
4. Return chicken to the skillet. Cook 4 more minutes per side, or until
done (internal temperature 170°F).
Serving suggestion: Serve chicken and sauce with cucumber slices
and long-grain and wild rice. Refrigerate leftovers. Makes 4 servings.
Note: To substitute Tyson Individually Fresh Frozen Boneless, Skinless
Chicken Breasts, simply increase the cooking time by about one-third.

YOSHIDA
Gourmet Chicken

Nonstick cooking spray
1 ¹/₂ pounds boneless, skinless chicken breasts
³/₄ cup Mr. Yoshida's Original Gourmet Sauce

1. Coat a medium skillet with cooking spray and heat over medium heat. Add chicken, cover and reduce heat. Cook, turning several times, until nearly cooked through.
2. Drain liquid from the pan and return to the heat. Add Gourmet Sauce and turn chicken to coat evenly. Cook, covered, for 10 minutes, turning chicken often to coat evenly.
3. Remove cover and cook for 5 minutes to reduce sauce to a glaze. Makes 4 servings.

JENNIE-O TURKEY STORE
Sesame Turkey Stir-Fry

3 tablespoons toasted sesame oil
¹/₄ cup sesame seeds
3 ounces (²/₃ cup) cashews, halved or whole
2 large red bell peppers, cut in ¹/₂-by-2-inch strips
2 large yellow bell peppers, cut in ¹/₂-by-2-inch strips
2 large green bell peppers, cut in ¹/₂-by-2-inch strips
3 large leeks, diced
1 ¹/₂ pounds Jennie-O Turkey Store* Golden Roast Turkey Breast, cut in ¹/₂-by-3-inch strips
Salt and pepper
8 cups cooked rice

1. Heat oil over medium heat in a large skillet or wok. Add sesame seeds and cashews; stir-fry for 2-4 minutes, or until toasted.
2. Add peppers and leeks; stir-fry for 2-5 minutes. Stir in turkey and cook for 3-6 minutes, or until vegetables are crisp-tender. Season to taste with salt and pepper.
3. Serve over warm rice. Makes 8-10 servings.

Note: Jennie-O Turkey Store VIP Turkey Breast or Premium Seasoned Turkey Breast can also be used.

* Brands may vary by region; substitute a similar product.

Entrées |

KIRKLAND SIGNATURE
Ginger Stir-Fry ▼

8 ounces beef, pork, chicken, turkey or shrimp
1/4 cup oil
2 tablespoons chopped fresh ginger
2 garlic cloves, cut in half
2 pounds Kirkland Signature Stir Fry Vegetables
1/4 cup roasted nuts (cashews, peanuts or almonds), optional
Salt and pepper

MARINADE
Beef or pork – 1/4 cup dry red wine, 3 tablespoons soy sauce
Chicken, turkey or shrimp – 1/4 cup dry white wine,
   3 tablespoons soy sauce

1. If using meat or poultry, cut in bite-size pieces. If using shrimp, cut in half lengthwise. Place in a bowl with marinade; mix well.

2. Heat oil in a wok or large skillet over high heat. Add ginger and garlic and cook for 30 seconds. Add vegetables and meat, poultry or shrimp; cook for 2 minutes. Stir in nuts, remove from heat, and season with salt and pepper to taste.

3. Discard garlic and serve immediately. Serve over rice or noodles if desired. Makes 4-6 servings.

KIRKLAND Signature

FOSTER FARMS
Thai Chicken with Basil ▲

4 Foster Farms* Boneless, Skinless Chicken Breast Fillets
1 teaspoon oil
1 ¼ cups chopped shiitake mushrooms
1 large garlic clove, minced
⅛ teaspoon red pepper flakes
2 teaspoons grated lime peel
3 ½ tablespoons oyster sauce
½ cup chopped basil
1 cup jasmine rice, cooked according to package directions
Basil leaves

1. Slice chicken into strips.
2. Heat oil in a large nonstick frying pan over medium heat.
Add mushrooms, garlic and red pepper flakes; cook for 3 minutes,
stirring frequently; remove from pan.
3. Add chicken strips to the pan and cook for 3-5 minutes, or until
nearly done.
4. Return mushroom mixture to the pan; add grated lime peel, oyster
sauce and chopped basil. Heat through, about 3 minutes more.
5. Place cooked rice on a serving platter, top with chicken mixture
and garnish with basil leaves. Makes 4 servings.

* Brands may vary by region; substitute a similar product.

FOSTER FARMS
Crispy Chicken ▲

6 cups cornflakes
1 tablespoon salt
1 tablespoon pepper
8-10 pieces Foster Farms* bone-in chicken
   (split breasts, drumsticks or thighs)
1 cup butter, melted
2 eggs, beaten

1. Preheat oven to 400°F.
2. Place cornflakes in a large zipper-lock bag and seal. Crush cornflakes
with a rolling pin. Add salt and pepper to cornflakes and shake. Set aside.
3. Roll chicken pieces in melted butter, then egg. Coat chicken pieces with
crushed cornflakes. Place in a nonstick baking dish.
4. Bake for 45 minutes, or until chicken reaches an internal temperature
of 170°F and is no longer pink inside. Makes 4-6 servings.

* Brands may vary by region; substitute a similar product.

DEL MONTE
Chicken and Peaches Picante ▼

1 15-ounce can S&W® Natural Style Sliced Peaches
4 boneless, skinless chicken breast halves
Salt and pepper
1 tablespoon olive oil
1/2 cup diced red bell pepper
1/2 cup thick and chunky salsa
1 tablespoon frozen orange juice concentrate
2 tablespoons chopped fresh cilantro or parsley

1. Drain peaches, reserving liquid; set aside.

2. Season chicken with salt and pepper to taste. Heat oil in a large nonstick skillet over medium-high heat. Add chicken and cook for 9-10 minutes, turning once, or until no longer pink in the center. Remove to a platter.

3. Add bell pepper to the skillet; reduce heat and stir-fry for 2 minutes, or until tender-crisp. Add reserved peach liquid, salsa and orange juice concentrate. Bring to a boil, scraping up browned bits from the pan. Add peaches and cilantro; cook and stir for 3 minutes, or until hot.

4. Spoon sauce and peaches over chicken and serve. Makes 4 servings.

Brands may vary by region; substitute a similar product.

McCORMICK
Mediterranean Marinated Chicken ▲

$^1/_3$ cup oil
3 tablespoons vinegar
1 teaspoon McCormick* Italian Seasoning
1 teaspoon McCormick Garlic Powder
$^1/_4$ teaspoon McCormick Ground Black Pepper
1 teaspoon McCormick* Lemon & Pepper Seasoning Salt
1 tablespoon chopped sun-dried tomatoes
Dash of salt
1 pound boneless, skinless chicken breasts

1. Combine all ingredients except chicken in a large self-closing plastic bag. Add chicken, seal the bag and turn gently to coat with marinade. Refrigerate for 30 minutes, or longer for extra flavor.
2. Preheat grill. Remove chicken from marinade and discard the marinade. Grill chicken over medium heat for 6-7 minutes per side, or until done. Makes 4 servings.

* Brands may vary by region; substitute a similar product.

McCORMICK

FOSTER FARMS
Ground Turkey Lasagna

3 tablespoons olive oil
1 package (1 ¼ pounds) Foster Farms* Ground Turkey
¾ teaspoon salt
¼ teaspoon ground pepper
¼ teaspoon red pepper flakes
1 yellow onion, chopped
8 garlic cloves, minced
¾ cup dry red wine

1 28-ounce can crushed tomatoes
1 14-ounce can diced tomatoes
1 bunch fresh basil, chopped
2 medium green onions, sliced
½ cup Italian parsley, chopped
15 2-inch-wide lasagna noodles
4 cups shredded mozzarella cheese
1 cup shredded Parmesan cheese

1. In a 6-quart saucepan, heat 2 tablespoons oil over medium heat. Add ground turkey, salt, ground pepper and red pepper flakes. When turkey is no longer pink, stir in yellow onion and garlic. Cook until onion is tender, stirring occasionally. Add wine; cook until absorbed. Add tomatoes and bring to a boil. Reduce heat to keep sauce at a steady simmer; cook, uncovered, for 45 minutes, stirring occasionally. Remove from heat; stir in basil, green onions, parsley and remaining oil. Add salt to taste.

2. Preheat oven to 400°F. Cook lasagna noodles according to package directions.

3. Spoon 1 cup sauce into a 9-by-13-inch baking pan. Arrange 4 cooked noodles side by side lengthwise in the pan; place 1 noodle crosswise at end of pan (trim as needed). Top with 2 cups sauce, ⅓ of mozzarella and ⅓ of Parmesan. Make 2 more layers, ending with cheese.

4. Bake until the top begins to brown and lasagna is hot, about 40 minutes. Let stand for 10 minutes before cutting. Makes 8 servings.

Brands may vary by region; substitute a similar product.

Foster Farms

BISQUICK
Chicken Salsa Fiesta ▲

²/₃ cup Original Bisquick mix
2 tablespoons water
1 egg
1 ¹/₂ cups shredded Cheddar cheese, divided
3 boneless, skinless chicken breast halves, cut in ¹/₂-inch pieces
2 teaspoons vegetable oil
1 ¹/₄ cups Old El Paso* Thick 'n Chunky Salsa

1. Preheat oven to 400°F. Coat an 8- or 9-inch square pan with nonstick cooking spray.
2. In a small bowl, stir together Bisquick, water and egg. Spread in the pan; sprinkle with 1 ¹/₄ cups of the cheese.
3. Cook and stir chicken in oil over medium-high heat until outsides turn white; drain. Stir in salsa; heat until hot. Spoon over batter in the pan to within ¹/₂ inch of edges.
4. Bake 22-25 minutes, or until edges are dark golden brown. Sprinkle with remaining cheese. Bake for 1-3 minutes, or until the cheese melts; loosen from sides of pan. Makes 6 servings.

High altitude: Increase first bake time to 25-30 minutes.

Brands may vary by region; substitute a similar product.

CLASSICO
Classic Two-Sauce Lasagna ▲

1 pound bulk Italian sausage or ground beef
1 15-ounce container ricotta cheese
1 10-ounce package frozen chopped spinach, thawed and drained
2 cups (8 ounces) shredded mozzarella cheese
4 tablespoons grated Parmesan cheese, divided
2 eggs
1 32-ounce jar Classico* Tomato Basil Pasta Sauce
12 no-bake lasagna noodles
1 16-ounce jar Classico* Alfredo Pasta Sauce

1. Preheat oven to 350°F. Brown sausage in a skillet, stirring until crumbly; drain. Combine ricotta, spinach, mozzarella, 2 tablespoons Parmesan and eggs in a bowl and mix well.
2. Spread 1 cup of the tomato sauce evenly over the bottom of a 9-by-13-inch baking dish. Layer 4 lasagna noodles, half of the cheese mixture, 1 cup tomato sauce and half of the cooked sausage over the tomato sauce. Continue layering with 4 lasagna noodles, the remaining cheese mixture, 1 cup tomato sauce, the remaining cooked sausage and the remaining 4 lasagna noodles. Spread Alfredo sauce evenly over the top. Sprinkle with 2 tablespoons Parmesan.
3. Bake, covered, for 40 minutes. Remove the cover and bake for 15 minutes, or until bubbly. Let stand for 10 minutes. Makes 10-12 servings.

Brands may vary by region; substitute a similar product.

CIBO NATURALS/MONTEREY PASTA
Quick and Easy Spinach Pesto Lasagna ▲

1 22-ounce jar Kirkland Signature by Cibo Naturals Pesto Sauce
1 cup whipping cream
1 36-ounce package Monterey Pasta Spinach and Cheese Ravioli
1 pound mozzarella cheese, shredded

1. Preheat oven to 350°F.
2. In a mixing bowl, blend pesto sauce with cream. Place a small amount of sauce in a 9-by-13-inch baking pan and spread evenly.
3. Place a single layer of ravioli evenly over the sauce. Spread 3/4 to 1 cup sauce evenly over ravioli and smooth with a rubber spatula. Sprinkle a quarter of the mozzarella evenly over the surface.

4. Repeat step 3, being sure to get even coverage for each layer.
5. Repeat the process one more time, using all of the remaining sauce and mozzarella to provide a thicker final topping. This will give the lasagna a nicely browned, bubbly appearance.
6. Bake the lasagna, uncovered, for 20-30 minutes, or until the top is lightly browned. Let stand for 5 minutes before cutting. Makes 6-8 servings.
Tip: For variety, add 1/2 cup each sliced zucchini and carrots in each layer. Vegetables should be sliced 1/8 to 1/4 inch thick.

KIRKLAND SIGNATURE
Meat Lasagna with Fresh Tossed Salad ▼

DIJON VINAIGRETTE
1 cup extra-virgin olive oil
¹/₂ cup balsamic vinegar
¹/₄ cup Dijon mustard
¹/₄ teaspoon salt
¹/₂ teaspoon cracked black pepper
¹/₄ teaspoon sugar

Using a food processor or whisk, combine all ingredients and mix until blended. Keep refrigerated. Blend dressing together before each use. Makes about 1 ³/₄ cups of dressing, or 12 servings.

Serve Kirkland Signature Meat Lasagna with fresh rolls or a baguette from the Costco Bakery and a refreshing salad. Combine mixed salad greens, sliced tomatoes, whole black olives, sliced red onions, shredded Romano cheese and croutons in a large bowl. Toss with Dijon Vinaigrette.

KIRKLAND *Signature*

VALLEY FINE FOODS
Ravioli Antipasto Salad ▲

2 dozen Pasta Prima Spinach &
   Mozzarella Ravioli

¹/₂ cup salami or pepperoni
   cut in ¹/₂-inch cubes

1 green bell pepper, julienned

1 cup cherry tomatoes, halved

1 cup sliced mushrooms

¹/₃ cup sliced olives

¹/₄ red onion, slivered

¹/₄ cup sliced pepperoncini

1 6 ¹/₂-ounce jar marinated
   quartered artichoke hearts,
   drained

¹/₂ cup provolone or mozzarella
   cheese cut in ¹/₂-inch cubes

DRESSING

2 tablespoons Italian Herb Cheese
   Mix (included)

2 ¹/₂ teaspoons Dijon mustard

2 ¹/₂ tablespoons
   balsamic vinegar

¹/₄ cup extra-virgin olive oil

2 garlic cloves, minced

1 tablespoon thinly sliced
   fresh basil

Juice of ¹/₂ lemon

¹/₂ teaspoon salt

¹/₂ teaspoon pepper

1. Cook ravioli according to package directions. Remove ravioli from
boiling water and cool in cold water for 1 minute. Drain.

2. Whisk together dressing ingredients until well blended.

3. In a large bowl, toss ravioli, salami, vegetables, cheese and dressing.
Top with 2 tablespoons Italian Herb Cheese Mix. Makes 5 servings.

DENICE & FILICE
Penne Pasta with Peppers ▲

1 pound penne pasta

2 tablespoons Kirkland Signature olive oil

2 Denice & Filice red onions, cut in strips

3 green bell peppers, seeded and chopped

2 yellow bell peppers, seeded and chopped

2 red bell peppers, seeded and chopped

2 garlic cloves, chopped

1. Bring a large pot of lightly salted water to a boil. Add pasta and cook
for 8-10 minutes, or until al dente. Drain water from pasta and set aside.

2. Heat oil in a large skillet over medium heat. Add onions, bell peppers
and garlic, and sauté until tender, approximately 10 minutes.

3. Pour vegetable mixture over pasta and serve. Makes 4-6 servings.

NEW YORK STYLE SAUSAGE
Fettuccine Neapolitan ▼

1 pound New York Style Sausage* Italian sausage
1/4 cup olive oil
4 ounces butter
1 teaspoon chopped fresh garlic
1 tablespoon chopped shallots
10 mushrooms, sliced
1/4 cup white wine
3/4 cup heavy cream
1/2 cup diced fresh tomatoes
1 cup marinara sauce
1 tablespoon chopped fresh basil
1 pound fettuccine, cooked until al dente and drained
Grated Parmesan cheese

1. Remove sausages from casing and cook in olive oil in a skillet over medium heat until crumbled and browned.

2. Drain off the oil and add butter, garlic, shallots and mushrooms. Cook until tender and lightly browned.

3. Add wine and cook until reduced. Stir in heavy cream.

4. Add diced tomatoes, marinara sauce and basil; cook for 5 minutes on medium heat, stirring occasionally.

5. Pour over cooked fettuccine and garnish with grated Parmesan.

Makes 4-6 servings.

Brands may vary by region; substitute a similar product.

TARANTINO'S
Pasta Tarantino ▼

4 ounces pancetta or your favorite bacon, diced

1 medium yellow onion, finely diced

4 garlic cloves, minced

1 ½ pounds Tarantino's* Italian sausage, casings removed

1 cup dry red wine

3 cups diced plum tomatoes, fresh or canned

¼ cup tomato paste

1 cup minced flat-leaf parsley

1 pound dry penne pasta, cooked and drained according to package directions

1 cup shredded Parmesan cheese

1. In a large sauce pot over medium-high heat, sauté pancetta to brown and render the fat. Add onion and sauté to soften. Add garlic and sausage; cook for about 10 minutes, stirring constantly to break up the meat and brown evenly.

2. Stir in wine, tomatoes and tomato paste; simmer for 20 minutes. Add parsley and adjust the seasonings.

3. Combine the sauce with the pasta. Serve in pasta bowls topped with Parmesan. Makes 6-8 servings.

Recipe provided by Chef Urs Emmenegger, C.E.C.
*Brands may vary by region; substitute a similar product.

EAT SMART
Quick and Easy Pasta Toss ▲

2 tablespoons olive oil

$^1/_2$ pound Italian sausage, cut in 1-inch pieces

$^1/_2$ cup chopped red onion

1 cup Eat Smart* Garden Vegetables carrots, cut in half lengthwise

1 cup Eat Smart* Garden Vegetables snap peas

1 cup Eat Smart* Garden Vegetables broccoli, cut in small florets

2 14 $^1/_2$-ounce cans diced tomatoes with basil, garlic and oregano

8 ounces penne pasta, prepared according to package directions

$^1/_2$ cup $^1/_2$-inch cubes mozzarella cheese

$^1/_3$ cup pitted kalamata olives

$^1/_4$ cup shredded Parmesan cheese

1. Heat oil in a large frying pan over high heat. Add sausage, onion and carrots; cook, stirring often, for 5 minutes.

2. Lower heat; add snap peas and broccoli. Cook until crisp-tender, making sure vegetables do not lose their color. Add tomatoes, mixing well, and cook just until warm.

3. Place hot pasta in a large bowl. Pour sauce over pasta, then add mozzarella and olives; toss to coat.

4. Serve immediately or let cool to room temperature. Just before serving, sprinkle with Parmesan cheese. Makes 4 servings.

Tip: This is an easy, quick dinner to put together. Eliminate the cheese and sausage if you'd prefer a lighter dish.

Brands may vary by region; substitute a similar product.

WILCOX FARMS
Harvest Frittata

1 ¹/₂ cups sliced zucchini

1 cup fresh corn kernels, or
    1 cup canned whole-kernel corn, well drained

¹/₂ cup chopped red bell pepper

¹/₄ cup chopped onion

¹/₄ teaspoon dried oregano leaves, crushed

1 tablespoon water

4 Wilcox* eggs

¹/₄ cup Kirkland Signature skim milk

¹/₄ cup (1 ounce) shredded low-fat Cheddar cheese

1. Preheat broiler.

2. In a 10-inch nonstick ovenproof skillet, combine zucchini, corn, bell pepper, onion, oregano and water. Cover and cook over medium heat, stirring occasionally, until crisp-tender.

3. Thoroughly blend eggs and milk in a bowl. Pour over vegetables. Cook over low heat until eggs are almost set. Sprinkle with cheese. Broil about 6 inches from the heat until cheese is melted. Makes 2-4 servings.

Recipe contributed by American Egg Board.
* Brands may vary by region; substitute a similar product.

Since 1909
Wilcox
Family Farms

MOZZARELLA FRESCA
Mozzarella al Polenta

1 tablespoon olive oil

1 tablespoon minced shallots

1 garlic clove, minced

1 tablespoon chopped
    fresh thyme

¹/₂ tablespoon chopped
    fresh oregano

2 tomatoes, diced

Salt and pepper

¹/₄ cup vegetable oil

8-16 ounces prepared polenta

¹/₄ cup flour

1 8-ounce Mozzarella Fresca*
    fresh mozzarella cheese, sliced

4 leaves fresh basil, slivered

1. Preheat broiler.

2. Heat olive oil in a saucepan and sauté shallots over medium heat for 3 minutes. Add garlic and sauté for 30 seconds. Stir in thyme, oregano, tomatoes, and salt and pepper to taste; heat completely. Adjust seasonings and set aside.

3. Heat vegetable oil in a sauté pan. Slice polenta into 8 pieces. Dredge only top and bottom sides of polenta pieces in flour; pan-fry on medium-high heat until a golden crust forms.

4. Place polenta on a cookie sheet; top with tomato sauce and then mozzarella. Broil until cheese begins to melt but not brown. Garnish with basil. Makes 4-6 servings.

* Brands may vary by region; substitute a similar product.

Mozzarella Fresca
Family of Fresh Italian Cheeses

PETERSON'S
Easy Four-Cheese Pizza ▾

1 loaf ciabatta bread
1 garlic clove
2-3 tablespoons olive oil
6 tablespoons tomato sauce
1 small red onion, sliced thin
2 tablespoons chopped
   pitted olives
Salt
Coarsely ground pepper
2 ounces Emmi Emmental,
   sliced in thin 2-inch strips

2 ounces Frico Holland Gouda,
   shredded
2 ounces Denmark's Finest
   Creamy Havarti, shredded
2 ounces Rosenborg Blue,
   cut in $1/2$-inch cubes
A few pine nuts
A few basil leaves or
   sprigs of rosemary

1. Preheat oven to 425°F.
2. Cut ciabatta in half lengthwise. Rub garlic on each ciabatta half. Brush with olive oil, spread on tomato sauce, and add onions and half of olives. Season to taste with salt and pepper.
3. Cover with slices of Emmental. Then sprinkle evenly with shredded Gouda and Havarti. Top off with chunks of blue cheese. Sprinkle with pine nuts and the remaining olives.
4. Bake for 10-12 minutes, or until bubbling and golden brown. Cut into serving portions and garnish with basil or rosemary. Makes 2-3 servings.

CATTLEMEN'S
Barbecue Chicken Pizza

2 cups diced cooked chicken breast
1 1/2 cups Cattlemen's* Barbecue Sauce
1 tablespoon dried oregano leaves
2 12-inch unbaked pizza crusts
1/2 cup diced green bell peppers
1/2 cup sliced black olives
1 cup shredded mozzarella cheese
1 cup shredded Cheddar cheese

1. Preheat oven to 400°F.
2. Combine chicken, barbecue sauce and oregano in a large bowl; mix well.
3. Spread 1 1/4 cups barbecue chicken mixture over each pizza crust. Layer 1/4 cup peppers and 1/4 cup olives over chicken. Sprinkle 1/2 cup mozzarella and 1/2 cup Cheddar on top.
4. Bake for 15-18 minutes, or until crust is browned. Slice into wedges and serve immediately. Makes 8 servings.

Brands may vary by region; substitute a similar product.

ConAgra
Turkey Club Pizza

1 13.8-ounce package refrigerated pizza crust dough
Pam No-Stick Cooking Spray
1/4 cup Hunt's Tomato Paste
1/4 cup mayonnaise
1/4 cup prepared pesto
1 cup (4 ounces) shredded Monterey Jack cheese
1 14 1/2-ounce can whole peeled tomatoes, drained, sliced
10 slices Armour* Ready Crisp Bacon, coarsely chopped
4 slices Butterball Hearty Thick Sliced Turkey Breast (4 ounces), cut in 1/2-inch-wide strips
1 cup (4 ounces) shredded Swiss cheese

1. Preheat oven to 400°F.
2. Unroll pizza crust dough on a baking sheet sprayed with cooking spray. Spread dough to edges of sheet to form a rectangular-shaped crust.
3. Combine tomato paste and mayonnaise in a small bowl. Spread evenly over the dough to within 1/2 inch of the edges. Top with pesto and spread evenly. Top with remaining ingredients.
4. Bake for 15-18 minutes, or until the crust is golden brown and the cheese is melted. Makes 6 servings.

Brands may vary by region; substitute a similar product.

ConAgra Foods®

TILLAMOOK
Vegetarian Quesadillas ▼

1 teaspoon oil
6-8 small flour tortillas
¼ cup mashed ripe avocado
1 cup chopped cooked artichoke hearts
¼ cup sliced green chiles
8 ounces Tillamook* Medium Cheddar Cheese, shredded
½ cup sour cream
1 ½ cups salsa

1. Heat oil at low to medium heat in a pan large enough to fit a flat tortilla.
2. Spread avocado, artichoke hearts and chiles evenly on tortilla. Sprinkle with cheese.
3. Place another tortilla on top and brown as cheese melts. Flip tortilla over using a large spatula; repeat heating process.
4. Cut quesadilla into 4 to 6 pie-shaped pieces. Top each slice with a dab of sour cream and salsa. Makes 4 servings.

Brands may vary by region; substitute a similar product.

Tillamook®

Entrées ▌

HEBREW NATIONAL
Three-Bean and Franks Bake ▲

1 tablespoon vegetable oil
1 medium onion, chopped
2 garlic cloves, minced
1 red bell pepper, seeded and coarsely chopped
1 green bell pepper, seeded and coarsely chopped
1 16-ounce can vegetarian baked beans
1 16-ounce can butter or lima beans, drained
1 16-ounce can red or kidney beans, drained
1/2 cup ketchup
1/2 cup packed light brown sugar
2 tablespoons cider vinegar
1 tablespoon deli mustard
1 12-ounce package Hebrew National* Beef Franks or Reduced Fat Beef Franks, cut in 1-inch pieces

1. Preheat oven to 350°F.

2. Heat oil in a large saucepan over medium heat; add onion and garlic and cook for 8 minutes, stirring occasionally. Add bell peppers and cook for 5 minutes, stirring occasionally. Stir in beans, ketchup, brown sugar, vinegar and mustard; bring to a boil. Stir in franks.

3. Transfer to a 2-quart casserole or 9-inch square baking dish. Bake for 40-45 minutes, or until hot and bubbly. Makes 6 main-dish or 10 side-dish servings.

Brands may vary by region; substitute a similar product.

CARANDO
Smoked Sausage Skillet ▲

1 tablespoon oil
1 large onion, thinly sliced
2 garlic cloves, minced
1 medium apple, cored and chopped
1 teaspoon dried rosemary
1 teaspoon dried sage
1 14 1/2-ounce can diced tomatoes
1 15-ounce can great northern beans, drained and rinsed
1 10-ounce package frozen lima beans, thawed
1 cup chicken broth
2 tablespoons tomato paste
1 pound Carando* Polska Kielbasa, cut into 6 pieces
1 1/2 cups seasoned croutons
1/3 cup fresh parsley, chopped

1. Heat oil in a large, heavy skillet. Add onion and garlic; sauté over medium-high heat. Add apple, herbs, tomatoes, beans, chicken broth and tomato paste, stirring to blend well.

2. Add sausage. Bring to a boil, cover, reduce heat and simmer for 20-30 minutes, or until thoroughly heated.

3. Serve topped with croutons and chopped parsley. Makes 6 servings.

Brands may vary by region; substitute a similar product.

HILLSHIRE FARM
Jambalaya ▼

2 tablespoons butter or margarine

1 medium onion, chopped

1/3 cup chopped green bell pepper

1/3 cup chopped celery

1 tablespoon minced garlic

1 pound Hillshire Farm* Polska Kielbasa, cut in 1-inch slices
(or 1 pound Hillshire Farm* Lit'l Smokies)

2 cups chicken broth

1 14 1/2-ounce can tomatoes, diced, drained

1 cup converted rice

1 tablespoon Cajun seasoning

1. Melt butter in a heavy saucepan over high heat. Add onion, bell pepper, celery and garlic; sauté for 5 minutes.

2. Add kielbasa, chicken broth, tomatoes, rice and Cajun seasoning; mix well and bring to a boil. Lower heat, cover and simmer for 25 minutes, or until the rice is cooked.

3. Remove from the heat and let sit, covered, for 5 minutes before fluffing with a fork. Makes 4-5 servings.

Brands may vary by region; substitute a similar product.

SWIFT
BBQ Pork Sandwiches for a Crowd

6-7 pounds Swift Natural Pork Shoulder Blade (Boston) Roast
1 large onion, quartered
3 garlic cloves, halved
1 teaspoon salt
1/2 teaspoon pepper
2 cups water
2 18-ounce bottles hickory-smoked barbecue sauce
24 sandwich rolls

1. Cut pork into 3-inch chunks. Place pork, onion, garlic, salt, pepper and water in a large pot. Cover tightly, bring to a boil and cook slowly for 2 1/2- 2 3/4 hours, or until pork is fork tender. Let cool in juices. Shred with 2 forks.
2. Heat shredded pork and barbecue sauce in a large pan over medium heat, stirring occasionally, until heated through. Serve in sandwich rolls. Makes about 24 sandwiches.

Swift tip: BBQ Pork can be made ahead and frozen for up to 1 month for later use. Defrost in the refrigerator and gently reheat.

Swift & Company

EVERGOOD FINE FOODS
Louisiana Hot Link Sausage Sandwich ▲

1 pound (4 links) Evergood* Louisiana Brand Hot Link Sausage
1/4 cup thinly sliced red bell pepper
1/4 cup thinly sliced yellow bell pepper
1/4 cup thinly sliced orange bell pepper
4 of your favorite French or sourdough rolls
4 tablespoons cole slaw
4 tablespoons barbecue sauce
4 tablespoons gourmet corn relish

1. Preheat grill.
2. Grill sausages and peppers over medium-high heat for 10 minutes, turning occasionally.
3. Warm or toast rolls.
4. Place each sausage in a roll and top with mixed peppers, 1 tablespoon cole slaw, 1 tablespoon barbecue sauce and 1 tablespoon corn relish. Makes 4 servings.

* Brands may vary by region; substitute a similar product.

EVERGOOD
FINE FOODS
SINCE 1926

VIE DE FRANCE
French Cheesesteak ▲

1 tablespoon butter
1 small yellow onion, sliced
Salt and pepper
1 large Vie de France* butter croissant
Mayonnaise
4 ounces sliced roast beef
1 ounce roasted red bell peppers, sliced
2 ounces Brie cheese

1. Melt butter in a sauté pan; add onions and salt and pepper to taste. Cook over low heat until onions begin to caramelize; remove from the heat.
2. Using a serrated knife, slice the croissant three-quarters of the way through, making sure to leave a spine. Spread mayonnaise over the bottom half of the croissant.
3. Place roast beef on a plate or pan and top with onions, roasted red bell peppers and Brie. Place in a microwave for 45 seconds or under a broiler until cheese melts. Carefully transfer the roast beef/cheese assembly to the bottom half of the croissant. Serve with a pickle spear and French fries. Makes 1 serving.

Brands may vary by region; substitute a similar product.

LA BREA BAKERY
Black Forest Ham and Gruyère on Ciabatta Sandwich Roll ▲

1 large red onion, thinly sliced
3 tablespoons extra-virgin olive oil
5 tablespoons balsamic vinegar
1/4 teaspoon kosher salt
Freshly ground pepper
1/4 cup Dijon mustard
1/2 cup mayonnaise
4 La Brea Bakery* Ciabatta Sandwich Rolls
12-16 slices (1 pound) Black Forest ham
8 slices Gruyère cheese (or Swiss or Emmentaler)
1 cup arugula

1. Place onions in a medium bowl. Pour oil and vinegar over onions; sprinkle with salt and pepper to taste. Toss to coat. Let marinate for at least 1/2 hour and up to 24 hours.
2. Preheat oven to 350°F. Spread onions in a thin layer on a baking sheet; pour remaining liquid over the onions. Bake for 10 minutes. Let cool.
3. Mix mustard and mayonnaise in a small bowl. Set aside.
4. Slice rolls in half and spread 2 tablespoons of dressing on each side. Layer ham, cheese, arugula and 3 tablespoons of onions on bottom half of rolls; cover with top half. Makes 4 servings.

Brands may vary by region; substitute a similar product.

SHADY BROOK FARMS
Zesty Rotisserie-Style Turkey Breast and Grilled Vegetable Panini Sandwich ▲

4 slices ciabatta Italian bread

1 tablespoon extra-virgin olive oil

8 ounces Shady Brook Farms* Zesty Rotisserie-Style
    Turkey Breast, sliced

1 cup grilled zucchini slices

1 cup sliced grilled red and yellow bell peppers

2 tablespoons roasted garlic mayonnaise or plain mayonnaise

1. Halve the ciabatta slices; brush the outside of each slice lightly with olive oil.

2. Fill each sandwich with 2 ounces sliced turkey breast and $1/4$ of the grilled vegetables. Drizzle mayonnaise over the vegetables. Place the top on each sandwich.

3. Preheat a skillet or griddle on medium-high. Grill sandwiches for 1 $1/2$ minutes per side with a weight on top. Makes 4 servings.

Brands may vary by region; substitute a similar product.

MILTON'S
Chicken Salad Sandwich ▲

20 ounces diced cooked chicken

$1/3$ cup diced celery

$1/3$ cup diced onion

$1/3$ cup diced red bell pepper

1 cup mayonnaise

$1/4$ teaspoon white pepper

$1/4$ teaspoon onion powder

$1/4$ teaspoon garlic powder

$1/2$ cup chopped pistachios

$1/2$ cup diced seedless grapes

8 slices Milton's Healthy Multi-Grain Bread

1. In a bowl, combine chicken, celery, onion, bell pepper, mayonnaise, white pepper, onion powder, garlic powder, pistachios and grapes.

2. Spread salad on the bread. Serve as whole sandwiches or cut into quarters for easy entertaining. Makes 4 servings.

MAPLE LEAF
Bacon Club Croissant ▲

6 strips Maple Leaf bacon

2 tablespoons mayonnaise

2 croissants, sliced in half

4 thin slices red onion

2 lettuce leaves

4 slices tomato, 1/4 inch thick

Salt and pepper

1 avocado, pitted, peeled and sliced

6 slices roast turkey

1. Cook bacon in a heavy skillet over medium-high heat until crisp, about 8 minutes. Transfer to paper towels.

2. Spread mayonnaise on croissants. Top the bottom half of each croissant with onion, lettuce and tomato.

3. Sprinkle tomato with salt and pepper to taste. Top with avocado, turkey and bacon. Makes 2 servings.

COSTCO DELI AND BAKERY
Turkey and Jarlsberg Flatbread Rollers ▲

Convenience and quality all wrapped into one—Costco Deli's ready-made Turkey and Jarlsberg Lahvash Flatbread Rollers give you a gourmet sandwich shop experience. Jarlsberg cheese is all natural, with a distinctive mellow, nutty flavor and creamy texture that is delicious in sandwiches made with Damascus Bakeries Fat Free Lahvash Flatbread.

The possibilities are endless. Slice thinly into pinwheels for the perfect-size hors d'oeuvres. Accompany with sliced fresh fruit for a light, healthy lunch. Or for heartier fare, serve with potato, pasta or macaroni salad and coleslaw.

Whatever the occasion—a trip to the beach, a backyard barbecue, lunch at the office, any festive event—Turkey and Jarlsberg Lahvash Flatbread Rollers make it special.

Look for Jarlsberg wedges and sliced Jarlsberg Lite in the Costco Deli section. Look for Damascus Bakeries Lahvash Flatbreads—now available in reduced carbs, too—in select Costco Bakery sections.

BC HOT HOUSE
Beefsteak Tomato, Bocconcini and Balsamic Stuffed Pita ▼

1 tablespoon balsamic vinegar
1 tablespoon chopped fresh basil
1 teaspoon minced garlic
2 tablespoons olive oil
Salt and pepper
3 large BC Hot House* beefsteak tomatoes, chopped
4 bocconcini (bite-size mozzarella balls), sliced
2 cups chopped head lettuce
2 large pita breads
Basil sprigs

1. Place vinegar, chopped basil and garlic in a mixing bowl. Drizzle in oil, whisking constantly, until smooth and thick. Season to taste with salt and pepper. Add tomatoes and bocconcini and toss well to coat. Let rest for at least 5 minutes. Add lettuce and toss to coat.

2. Cut pitas in half. Open each half to form a pocket. Fill with $1/4$ of the salad mixture, garnish with a sprig of basil and place in the middle of a folded napkin. Repeat with the remaining mixture and serve immediately. Makes 4 servings.

Brands may vary by region; substitute a similar product.

BUMBLE BEE
Caesar Bistro Wraps ▲

6 10- to 12-inch tortillas
1 cup herbed spreadable cheese
4 cups shredded romaine lettuce
2 6-ounce cans Bumble Bee* Solid White
   Albacore Tuna in water, drained
2 cups seeded and diced tomatoes
1/2 cup bottled Caesar salad dressing
1/2 cup shredded Parmesan cheese

1. Spread each tortilla with spreadable cheese to within 2 inches of edges. Sprinkle romaine evenly over the lower half of each tortilla.
2. In a bowl, toss together tuna, tomatoes and dressing. Spoon over the lettuce on each tortilla. Sprinkle with Parmesan.
3. Roll the tortillas burrito-style by folding over the sides toward the filling and then rolling from bottom to top to seal. Cut in half to serve. Makes 6 servings.

* Brands may vary by region; substitute a similar product.

JIF
Peanut Vegetable Curry Wraps ▲

2 tablespoons Crisco* Vegetable or Canola Oil
3-4 garlic cloves, minced
1 cup chopped onions
1 tablespoon curry powder
3/4 cup chopped cauliflower
3/4 cup chopped broccoli
1/2 cup shredded carrots
Salt and pepper
1/2 cup chopped ripe tomatoes
1/2 cup Jif* Creamy Peanut Butter
6-8 flour tortillas or chapatis
Plain yogurt or sour cream
2-3 green onions, chopped

1. Heat Crisco oil in a large skillet over medium heat. Add garlic and onions and cook, stirring often, until just tender but not browned. Stir in curry powder and cook for 1 minute.
2. Add cauliflower, broccoli, carrots, and salt and pepper to taste. Cover and cook for 4-5 minutes, or until the vegetables are just tender. Stir in tomatoes and Jif peanut butter. Cook, uncovered, for about 1 minute.
3. To serve, put filling in tortillas and roll up. Garnish with yogurt and green onions. Makes 3-4 servings.

* Brands may vary by region; substitute a similar product.

Entrées I

TANIMURA & ANTLE
Romaine Caesar Wraps ▼

2 heads Tanimura & Antle* romaine hearts

2 cups cubed cooked chicken (approx. 2 8-ounce boneless chicken breasts)

1 cup shredded Parmesan cheese

1/2 small red onion, thinly sliced

1 cup creamy Caesar dressing

8 9-inch flour tortillas, plain or flavored

1. Chop romaine hearts into bite-size pieces; place in a large bowl. Add chicken, cheese, onion and dressing; toss well to coat.

2. Soften tortillas in microwave oven (about 20 seconds on high).

3. To make wrap, place tortilla on plate and spoon Caesar salad along the center. Drizzle with additional dressing if desired. Roll tortilla from one side, burrito style, folding the bottom up and in to hold in the salad.

4. Repeat for remaining tortillas. Makes 4 servings.

Creative ideas:

1. Try leftover rotisserie, barbecued or fried chicken for a convenient change of pace.

2. Use your favorite ranch or honey mustard dressing in place of Caesar.

Brands may vary by region; substitute a similar product.

KIRKLAND SIGNATURE
Classic Chicken Caesar Salad Wraps ▲

Kirkland Signature* Chicken Caesar Salad, croutons removed
8 10-inch flour tortillas
16 pieces crisp cooked bacon

1. Preheat oven to 325°F.
2. Place salad in a bowl, squeeze lemons over the salad and toss with half of the provided dressing.
3. Divide tortillas into groups of 4 and seal in foil packages. Place packets in the oven for about 20 minutes. (For a real treat, heat the tortillas for about 20 seconds on each side over medium coals on the barbecue.)
4. Spread some of the reserved dressing on each warm tortilla, add the salad, tuck in the sides and roll up like a cigar. For an added treat, place 2 pieces of bacon in each tortilla before rolling up. Cut in half diagonally. Makes 8 tortilla wraps.

Brands may vary by region; substitute a similar product.

NEW YORK APPLE/RICE FRUIT
Tuna Apple Tortilla Wraps ▲

2 flour tortillas
2 tablespoons herbed cream cheese, puréed roasted peppers or hummus
1 large Empire or fresh Eastern Apple,* cored and thinly sliced
1 6-ounce can tuna in water, drained
1 tablespoon reduced-fat mayonnaise or sour cream
Ground pepper, to taste
Mild curry powder, optional
2 green onions, cut in half, sliced lengthwise

1. Spread each tortilla with 1 tablespoon of spread. Arrange apple slices down the center of the tortillas to within 1 inch of the edges.
2. Flake the tuna into a small bowl and combine with mayonnaise and pepper. Spoon tuna mixture over the apple slices. Sprinkle with mild curry powder, if desired. Top with green onions.
3. Roll the wraps from front to back. Makes 2 wraps.

Recipe provided by Olwen Woodier, from The Apple Cookbook (Storey Books, 2001).
Brands may vary by region; substitute a similar product.

Eastern Apples
CRISPIER • JUICIER • TASTIER

FOSTER FARMS
Chicken Salad with Fennel, Orange and Raspberries ▼

*TANGY RASPBERRY-
   ORANGE DRESSING*

3 tablespoons olive oil

3 tablespoons grainy mustard

3 tablespoons honey

2 tablespoons raspberry vinegar

Grated peel and juice of 1 large
   navel orange

1/2 teaspoon salt

1/4 teaspoon freshly
   ground pepper

SALAD

4 Foster Farms* boneless, skinless
   chicken breast fillets

1/2 cup orange juice

3 large navel oranges

1 fennel bulb, trimmed and
   coarsely diced

8 cups mixed greens

1 small red onion, thinly sliced

1/4 cup raspberries

1. Prepare Tangy Raspberry-Orange Dressing: In a medium bowl, whisk together all ingredients.

2. In a large frying pan over medium-high heat, spoon 2 tablespoons of Tangy Raspberry-Orange Dressing. Place chicken in the pan and sauté until golden brown. Turn breasts over and add orange juice; bring to a simmer and reduce heat to low. Cover and cook for 20 minutes, or until chicken is no longer pink inside or internal temperature is 160°F.

3. Peel oranges and slice into rounds. Place fennel and mixed greens in a large bowl. Reserve 2 tablespoons of the dressing and toss the remainder with the greens. Arrange on 4 chilled dinner plates.

4. Slice chicken into thin strips and place with orange slices and onions on top of greens. Drizzle with reserved dressing and sprinkle raspberries on top. Makes 4 servings.

* Brands may vary by region; substitute a similar product.

CHELAN FRESH
Crunchy Apple-Chicken Salad ▲

3 ¹/₂ cups diced Chelan Fresh* Granny Smith apples

2 tablespoons lemon juice

2 cups grapes

1 celery stalk, diced

1 large carrot, shredded

3 cups chopped romaine lettuce

12 ounces canned chicken breast

¹/₃ cup walnut pieces

¹/₂ cup nonfat mayonnaise

2 tablespoons nonfat sour cream

1. In a large bowl, mix apples with lemon juice. Stir in grapes, celery, carrot, romaine, chicken and walnuts.

2. In a small bowl, combine mayonnaise and sour cream. Add to the salad, stirring to mix well. Makes 6-8 servings.

Brands may vary by region; substitute a similar product.

SEALD SWEET
Orange Pepper Salad ▲

2 medium bell peppers, thinly sliced

4 cups shredded cabbage

²/₃ cup ranch dressing

¹/₄ cup frozen Florida orange juice concentrate, thawed

12 ounces cooked beef or poultry

4 cups Seald Sweet* fresh Florida orange sections

1 bag salad greens

1. In a salad bowl, combine peppers and cabbage.

2. In a small bowl, stir together ranch dressing and thawed juice concentrate; toss with the peppers and cabbage.

3. Cut or shred beef or poultry into thin bite-size strips. Fold meat and orange sections into the peppers and cabbage. Serve on a bed of salad greens. Makes 4-6 servings.

Brands may vary by region; substitute a similar product.

Seald⊛Sweet

KIRKLAND SIGNATURE
Chicken Noodle Salad with Spicy Peanut Butter

1 12 1/2-ounce can Kirkland Signature Chunk Chicken Breast
6 tablespoons creamy peanut butter
3 tablespoons rice vinegar
3 tablespoons soy sauce
1 1/2 tablespoons sugar
1 tablespoon Asian sesame oil
1 tablespoon minced peeled fresh ginger

1/2 teaspoon cayenne pepper
8 ounces linguine
1 large orange bell pepper, cut in matchstick-size strips
1/2 cup chopped green onions
5 large lettuce leaves
1/4 cup fresh cilantro, chopped
1/4 cup salted peanuts, chopped

1. Drain chicken, reserving broth.

2. Combine 1/4 cup of the reserved broth, peanut butter, vinegar, soy sauce, sugar, sesame oil, ginger and cayenne in a small bowl; whisk to blend.

3. Cook linguine in a large pot of boiling salted water until tender. Drain pasta, rinse with cold water and drain again.

4. Transfer pasta to a medium bowl. Add chicken, bell pepper and green onions. Pour dressing over; toss to coat.

5. Line a serving bowl with lettuce leaves. Transfer salad to the prepared bowl. Sprinkle with cilantro and peanuts. Makes 4 servings.

SHIITAKE-YA
Ramen Salad

3 cups dried Shiitake-Ya mushroom slices
1 cup shredded carrots
1 cucumber, thinly sliced
3 green onions, thinly sliced
2 cups cubed cooked chicken
1 11-ounce can mandarin oranges, drained
3 packages ramen noodles

1/4 cup white wine vinegar
2 tablespoons sugar
2 tablespoons vegetable oil
1 tablespoon soy sauce
1 1/2 teaspoons Asian sesame oil
1/2 teaspoon salt
1/4 teaspoon cayenne pepper
3/4 cup coarsely chopped salted peanuts

1. Pour boiling water over shiitake mushroom slices and cover for 30 minutes to rehydrate. Drain and squeeze out any excess water.

2. Place shiitake mushroom slices, carrots, cucumber, green onions, chicken and oranges in a large bowl.

3. Cook ramen according to package directions; rinse with cold water, drain and add to the bowl.

4. In a small bowl, whisk together vinegar, sugar, vegetable oil, soy sauce, sesame oil, salt and cayenne.

5. Sprinkle peanuts over the salad, add dressing and toss. Makes 4-6 servings.

Shiitake-Ya™

TANIMURA & ANTLE
Fiesta Lettuce Bowls ▼

1 pound lean ground beef or ground turkey
2 tablespoons chili powder
1 24-ounce jar salsa
1 16-ounce can pinto beans, drained
Salt and pepper
1 head Tanimura & Antle* iceberg lettuce
2 cups broken tortilla chips
Guacamole, optional
Cheddar cheese, shredded, optional

1. Brown meat with chili powder over medium heat in a large skillet. When almost done, stir in 1/2 cup salsa and beans; cook for 2 minutes. Season to taste with salt and pepper. Remove from heat and cool slightly.

2. Remove core and outer leaf from iceberg lettuce. Carefully peel off 4 whole leaves. Place leaves on serving plates to form lettuce bowls.

3. Chop remaining iceberg head into bite-size pieces and place in a large bowl. Add 1/2 cup salsa, meat mixture and tortilla chips; toss well. Spoon salad into lettuce bowls and serve immediately with additional salsa, guacamole and shredded cheese, if desired. Makes 4 servings.

Creative ideas:

1. Garnish Fiesta Lettuce Bowls with cilantro sprigs, sliced green onions, tomato wedges, ripe olives or a dollop of sour cream.

2. For vegetarian Fiesta Lettuce Bowls, use 1 cup diced Cheddar cheese and 2 cans vegetarian chili beans in place of meat mixture. Toss with iceberg lettuce and remaining ingredients.

Brands may vary by region; substitute a similar product.

CHICKEN OF THE SEA
Italian Caprese Bread Salad ▲

1 baguette, sliced ¼ inch thick (about 24 slices),
   toasted with olive oil and garlic
1 7-ounce bag European-style salad greens
¾ cup red wine vinaigrette or other dressing of choice
2 6-ounce cans Chicken of the Sea Chunk Light Tuna
   in spring water, drained
½ cup chopped Italian parsley
3 tablespoons capers, drained
1 cup diced plum tomatoes
1 cup cubed fresh mozzarella cheese
1 cup halved ripe olives
½ cup chopped fresh basil

1. Line each plate with 6 baguette slices.
2. Toss salad greens in a bowl with vinaigrette; divide evenly over
baguette slices.
3. Gently flake tuna into a bowl and toss with parsley and capers;
set aside.
4. Sprinkle tomatoes and mozzarella over salad greens. Top with
tuna and olives; garnish with basil. Makes 4 servings.

READY PAC
Grand Parisian Salad with
Grilled Beef Sirloin ▲

¼ cup minced shallots
3 tablespoons soy sauce
1 cup olive oil
1 tablespoon red wine vinegar
1 tablespoon chopped fresh thyme
Juice of 1 lemon
1 pinch salt and pepper
1 pound beef sirloin steak
1 16-ounce bag Ready Pac* Grand Parisian Salad

1. Combine shallots, soy sauce, oil, vinegar, thyme, lemon juice, salt
and pepper in a bowl or zipper-lock bag. Add sirloin and marinate
in the refrigerator for 2-3 hours.
2. Grill sirloin to desired doneness.
3. Place salad ingredients in a bowl and toss.
4. Cut sirloin into thin slices and serve over the salad. Makes 4 servings.
Tip: Ready Pac Grand Parisian Salad can also be served with your
favorite grilled fish or poultry.
* Brands may vary by region; substitute a similar product.

BABÉ FARMS
Spring Mix and Grilled Chicken
Salad with Salsa Vinaigrette ▼

SALSA VINAIGRETTE
3 medium plum tomatoes, chopped

3/4 cup chopped
   green bell pepper

1/3 cup chopped red onion

1 fresh jalapeño pepper, chopped

3 tablespoons red wine vinegar

2 teaspoons Dijon mustard

1/2 cup olive oil

3 tablespoons chopped
   fresh cilantro

3/4 teaspoon ground cumin

1/2 teaspoon salt

1/2 teaspoon black pepper

SALAD
8 cups Babé Farms* Spring Mix

1 1/2 pounds grilled boneless
   chicken, cut in julienne strips

1 large ripe avocado,
   peeled and sliced

1. To make the Salsa Vinaigrette, place all ingredients in a small bowl and stir to combine.

2. Place Spring Mix and chicken in a salad bowl and stir to combine. Pour dressing over the salad and toss. Arrange avocado slices in a decorative spiral over the salad. Makes 4 servings.

Brands may vary by region; substitute a similar product.

Celebrating the sensational salmon

Salmon
The Costco Way

The legendary salmon is delicious, versatile, nutritious—and easy to prepare. Try these recipes, submitted by Costco members, for your next special meal.

Dennis Anderson

Dennis Anderson of Danville, California, cooks salmon the Pacific way.

1 salmon fillet
1/4 cup chopped fresh dill, or 2 tablespoons dried dill
1/2 stick butter, melted
1 each lemon, lime and red onion, thinly sliced

Preheat a covered gas grill or use a pot grill with soaked wood chips for smoky flavor. Sprinkle salmon with dill. Drizzle with butter and cover with alternating slices of lemon, lime and red onion. Cook on covered grill for about 20 minutes; do not turn and do not overcook.

Donna Holt

Donna Holt of Chowchilla, California, remembers her mom's salmon patties, which were made from canned salmon. Now she makes them using Costco's frozen salmon.

Crumble up grilled salmon to equal 2 cups. Add 1/4 cup bread crumbs, 1 or 2 eggs, 1/2 onion, chopped, and salt and pepper. Mix together into a rolled ball and smush into patties. Fry in about 6 tablespoons hot oil. Drain on paper towel. Drizzle with olive oil and seasonings to taste. Makes 6 patties.

Michaelene Hearn

Michaelene Hearn of Clarkston, Michigan, reports, "I love Costco salmon!" Just cook the salmon fillet and add this sauce at the end and for dipping.

1 cup butter
6 tablespoons soy sauce
4 tablespoons ketchup
2 tablespoons Worcestershire sauce
4 garlic cloves, crushed
2 tablespoons Dijon mustard

Combine all ingredients in a small saucepan. Heat gently but thoroughly. Do not burn.

Suzanne Huening

Suzanne Huening of Royal Oak, Michigan, has streamlined salmon preparation!

"I wanted to submit one of my favorite recipe tips—so easy and so gourmet! We serve Vidalia onion vinaigrette as a sauce on salmon—either fresh or frozen. It enhances the flavor of the salmon and tastes like I fussed making a homemade sauce."

Ronnie Sklarin

Ronnie Sklarin of Albuquerque wanted to share this longtime family favorite.

2 pounds salmon fillet
16 ounces plain nonfat yogurt
2 tablespoons low-fat mayonnaise
1 pound green seedless grapes, thinly sliced
2 cucumbers, peeled and shredded

Grill or bake salmon. Combine yogurt and mayonnaise well. Add grapes and cucumber. Pour over salmon. Makes 4-6 servings.

Imelda Trinidad

Imelda Trinidad of Los Angeles has created a perfect pesto and salmon combination.

Salmon fillet
Salt and pepper
8-10 ounces pesto sauce
Pine nuts, chopped (optional)

Preheat oven to 350°F. Wash the salmon in running water and pat dry. Place in a rectangular glass baking dish. Season salmon with a dash of salt and pepper. Spread the pesto sauce generously over both sides of the fish. Add pine nuts if desired. Bake 20 minutes, or until salmon is barely opaque in the center. Makes 8 servings.

Plank Cooking

Plank cooking is part of the Pacific Northwest's heritage from Native Americans, who discovered that the flavor of salmon was enhanced by cooking the fish on wood planks from alder and cedar trees. Cooking over certain woods imbues a desirable smoky spice inside and outside food, as contemporary barbecue enthusiasts will attest. It's seasoning made simple.

The traditional art is revived with modern cedar and alder planks that are kiln dried and ready for use in the oven or on an outdoor grill, gas or charcoal. Soak the planks in water for 1 hour before use. No extra oil is required to prevent sticking. Planks designed for ovens last for several years; grill planks are intended for one use only.

MARINE HARVEST
Grilled Salmon ▾

4 salmon portions, 6-8 ounces each

1. Marinate salmon portions for ¹/₂ hour on the counter or 1 hour in the refrigerator (see accompanying recipes).

2. Preheat the grill.

3. When grilling, it helps to use an oiled fish and vegetable grill topper, with smaller holes, to prevent the fish from falling through. Place marinated fish on the hot grill and cook for approximately 5 minutes on each side. Make sure the fish flakes apart easily before removing.

4. Serve with fresh salsa (see recipe) or thoroughly heated leftover marinade.

MARINE HARVEST
Fresh Cucumber Salsa ▴

1 cucumber, peeled and diced
2 tablespoons finely chopped fresh cilantro
1 tablespoon finely chopped scallion greens
1 teaspoon finely chopped fresh jalapeño pepper (no seeds)
1 teaspoon natural sugar
1 tablespoon fresh lime juice

Mix all ingredients thoroughly in a nonreactive bowl.

MARINE HARVEST
Kentucky-Style Marinade ◀

$^1/_2$ **cup bourbon whiskey**
$^1/_3$ **cup soy sauce**
$^1/_4$ **cup brown sugar**
2 tablespoons red wine vinegar
3 tablespoons olive oil
2 tablespoons Dijon mustard
2 tablespoons minced garlic
1 tablespoon Worcestershire sauce

Mix all ingredients thoroughly in a nonreactive bowl.

MARINE HARVEST
New England-Style Marinade ▼

$^1/_3$ **cup fresh orange juice**
$^1/_3$ **cup pure maple syrup**
3 tablespoons balsamic vinegar
3 garlic cloves, minced
1 tablespoon light oil
1 tablespoon honey

Mix all ingredients thoroughly in a nonreactive bowl.

MARINE HARVEST
Florida-Style Marinade ▲

$^1/_3$ **cup orange juice**
2 tablespoons honey
2 tablespoons soy sauce
2 teaspoons fresh lemon juice
1 teaspoon minced fresh ginger, or $^1/_2$ teaspoon ground ginger
1 teaspoon chopped garlic

Mix all ingredients thoroughly in a nonreactive bowl.

FRESH FARMED ATLANTIC SALMON
Tuscan Salmon ▲

1 teaspoon each salt, dry mustard and dried thyme, crushed
1/2 teaspoon ground pepper
4 6-ounce Fresh Farmed Atlantic Salmon* fillets
2 teaspoons honey
3 teaspoons olive oil, divided
2 quarts (8 cups) spinach leaves, with large stems removed
1/2 teaspoon minced garlic
2 cups halved red California seedless grapes
1/2 cup dry red wine

1. Preheat oven to 300°F.
2. Combine salt, mustard, thyme and pepper in a small bowl. Rub salmon with honey and sprinkle with some of the seasoning mixture. Heat 2 teaspoons olive oil in a nonstick skillet. Brown both sides of salmon over medium-high heat.
3. Toss spinach and garlic with 1 teaspoon oil in a 9-by-13-inch baking dish. Place salmon on spinach, cover loosely with foil and bake for 10 minutes, or until salmon has an internal temperature of 130°F.
4. Sauté grapes briefly in the skillet. Add wine, bring to a boil and season to taste with remaining seasoning mixture and salt; continue cooking to reduce by half.
5. Serve salmon on spinach; top with grape sauce. Makes 4 servings.

Recipe provided by the California Table Grape Commission.
* Brands may vary by region; substitute a similar product.

AquaChile
Salmon with Pistachio-Basil Butter ▲

1/4 cup pistachios
10 large fresh basil leaves
1 garlic clove
1/2 cup butter, softened
1 teaspoon lime juice
Salt and pepper
Hot pepper sauce, optional
6 6-ounce portions fresh skinless salmon fillets
1/2 cup dry white wine, optional
Basil leaves, for garnish

1. Blend pistachios, basil leaves and garlic clove in a food processor until finely chopped. Add butter and lime juice; blend until incorporated into mixture. Season to taste with salt, pepper and hot sauce. Chill.
2. Preheat oven to 400°F.
3. Place salmon fillets in a buttered 9-by-13-inch baking dish in a single layer. Season to taste with salt and pepper. Bake until fillet tips are opaque, about 10 minutes.
4. Place 2 tablespoons pistachio-basil butter on each fillet. Pour wine into the pan. Continue baking until fillets are opaque in the center, about 5 minutes. Garnish with additional basil leaves and serve immediately. Makes 6 servings.

AquaChile

CAMANCHACA
Sensational Ginger/Honey Salmon ▼

3 ounces sake (Japanese rice wine)
2 tablespoons soy sauce
1 tablespoon finely chopped or julienned fresh ginger
Cracked pepper to taste
4 6-ounce fresh skinless, boneless Camanchaca* salmon portions
Honey to taste
Lemon or lime, optional
Lemon slices and parsley sprigs for garnish

1. Preheat broiler.

2. Mix together sake, soy sauce, ginger and cracked pepper; pour into a shallow casserole dish.

3. Pierce salmon portions with a fork and place in the casserole. Baste salmon with the marinade; drizzle generously with honey.

4. Place the casserole under the broiler on the top oven rack. Watch closely until the salmon begins to brown, approximately 3-5 minutes. Remove from the oven and turn the salmon. Baste with marinade and generously drizzle with honey. Continue broiling for 3-5 minutes, or until browned.

5. Squeeze a lemon or lime over the salmon if desired. Garnish with lemon slices and parsley sprigs. Serve with your favorite vegetables or rice.
Makes 4 servings.

* Brands may vary by region; substitute a similar product.

Entrées I

FISH HOUSE FOODS
Stuffed Salmon with Garlic-Tomato Confit and Asparagus Tips ▼

1 bunch medium asparagus

2 portions Kirkland Signature stuffed salmon entrée

Kosher salt

Freshly ground black pepper

3 garlic cloves, slivered

¼ cup extra-virgin olive oil

2 large tomatoes, peeled, seeded and diced

1 tablespoon julienned fresh basil leaves

1 lemon, thinly sliced

1 tablespoon thinly sliced fresh chives

1. Preheat broiler.

2. Cut 2-inch tips off the asparagus and blanch until tender; cool and reserve.

3. Season salmon with salt and pepper to taste. Broil salmon, taking care not to blacken or burn.

4. Cook garlic in olive oil in a medium saucepan over moderate heat just until garlic begins to brown. Remove from heat and stir in diced tomatoes, basil, and salt and pepper to taste. Stir in asparagus tips.

5. Place salmon and vegetables on plates and garnish with lemon slices and chives. Makes 2 servings.

FISH HOUSE FOODS, INC.
VISTA, CA 92083

TRIDENT SEAFOODS
Salmon Benedict with Dill Havarti

4 4-ounce Trident Seafoods Alaskan Salmon Burgers
Prepared Hollandaise sauce
1/4 teaspoon dried dill
2 plain English muffins, split
4 large eggs
4 slices dill Havarti cheese

1. Prepare ingredients simultaneously so that everything stays hot.

2. In a greased pan, cook salmon burgers from frozen over medium heat for 4-5 minutes on each side, or until cooked through.

3. Prepare Hollandaise sauce (fresh, premade or from a dry packet); stir in dill.

4. Lightly toast 4 halves of English muffins.

5. Prepare eggs by poaching or frying over easy.

6. Assemble in this order: English muffin half, salmon burger, cheese and egg; spoon Hollandaise sauce on top. Serve immediately. Makes 4 servings.

Tip: To cut cooking time in half (4-5 minutes), cook frozen salmon burgers in a George Foreman grill.

FJORD SEAFOOD USA
Skewered Salmon Slivers

1 tablespoon chopped
  fresh rosemary
2 tablespoons olive oil
1/2 cup lemon juice
1 garlic clove, crushed
1/4 cup dry sherry
1/4 teaspoon salt
1/4 teaspoon freshly cracked
  black pepper

1/4 teaspoon cayenne pepper
2 1/2 pounds fresh Kirkland
  Signature* skinless
  salmon fillets
12 bamboo skewers
12 small green and red bell
  pepper wedges
12 small onion wedges

1. In a bowl combine rosemary, olive oil, lemon juice, garlic, sherry, salt, pepper and cayenne.

2. Cutting from head to tail, slice salmon fillets into 1-by-4-inch strips. Place salmon strips in the marinade and refrigerate for 1 hour, turning several times.

3. Preheat grill.

4. Remove salmon from the marinade and shake dry; reserve marinade. Thread each salmon sliver lengthwise on a skewer, piercing it 2 or 3 times. Alternate with peppers and onions.

5. Brush the grill rack quickly with cooking oil. Arrange skewers in parallel lines 6 inches above the heat. Cook for 5 minutes; turn, brush with marinade and grill until salmon is just cooked through. Serve over rice. Makes 4 servings.

* Brands may vary by region; substitute a similar product.

Fjord Seafood USA

MAZZETTA
Grilled Lobster Tails ▲

4 Seamazz lobster tails
3 lemons
Salt and pepper to taste
1 pound butter
3 garlic cloves, crushed

1. Place lobster tails in a pan of cold water to thaw. Preheat grill.
2. Cut open the top of each lobster tail. Pull meat away from the shell, leaving meat attached at the tail end. Rinse lobster tail and place meat on top of the shell.

3. Sprinkle lobster meat with lemon juice, salt and pepper; place 1 pat of butter on each tail. Refrigerate until ready to cook.
4. Melt remaining butter in a small saucepan; add crushed garlic and simmer. Reserve half for basting and half for dipping.
5. Cook lobster tails on the grill over indirect heat, with the cover closed. Baste frequently with garlic butter. Lobster tails are done when the meat is opaque and firm to the touch, about 15-18 minutes.
6. Serve with lemon wedges and remaining garlic butter for dipping.
Makes 4 servings.

Mazzetta Company, LLC®

MAZZETTA
Mediterranean Shrimp ▼

1 pound Seamazz raw 21/25-count tail-on shrimp
1 ½ cups extra-virgin light olive oil
Juice of 1 lemon
1 teaspoon coarse sea salt
8 garlic cloves, sliced
½ teaspoon red pepper flakes
1 teaspoon chopped fresh parsley

1. Thaw shrimp according to package directions. Rinse shrimp and refrigerate until ready to use.
2. Heat olive oil and lemon juice in a heavy-duty Dutch oven. Add shrimp, salt, garlic and red pepper flakes. Bring to a boil, stirring occasionally, and cook for 3-4 minutes. Shrimp is done when meat is opaque and firm to the touch. Garlic slices will be browned.
3. Sprinkle shrimp with parsley and serve immediately. Makes 4 servings.

Mazzetta Company, LLC ®

ConAgra
Shrimp and King Crab Fettuccine with Olives and Artichokes ▲

4 tablespoons butter

3 garlic cloves, crushed through a press, or 1 1/2 teaspoons minced garlic

1 tablespoon minced shallot or onion

1 pound ConAgra* raw U-15 headless shrimp, peeled and deveined

1 teaspoon dried oregano

1 teaspoon garlic powder

1/4 cup chicken broth

8 ounces ConAgra* king crab meat, chopped

1 14-ounce can artichoke hearts, drained

1/4 cup sliced green olives, drained

1 2 1/4-ounce can sliced black olives, drained

8 ounces fettuccine, cooked and drained

1/4 cup grated Parmesan cheese

3 tablespoons chopped fresh parsley

1. Melt butter in a medium skillet over medium heat; add garlic, shallot, shrimp, oregano and garlic powder. Sauté for 1 minute.

2. Add chicken broth and bring to a boil. Stir in crab, artichokes and olives and heat through.

3. Toss with fettuccine. Garnish with Parmesan and parsley. Makes 4-6 servings.

Brands may vary by region; substitute a similar product.

MARGARITAVILLE SHRIMP
Shrimp in Cilantro Tomato Blush Sauce ▲

1 package (1 1/2 pounds) frozen Margaritaville Island Lime Shrimp

1 garlic clove, chopped

1 cup chopped tomatoes, fresh or canned

1 14 1/2-ounce can chicken broth

1/2 cup chopped cilantro, divided

1/2 cup light cream

1 teaspoon cornstarch

1 pound angel hair pasta or thin spaghetti, cooked and drained

1. In a large skillet over medium heat, sauté shrimp and garlic for 8-10 minutes, turning shrimp to cook evenly.

2. Add tomatoes, chicken broth and 1/4 cup cilantro. Bring to a boil, then reduce heat. In a bowl, blend cream with cornstarch; stir into shrimp and heat gently until sauce is slightly thickened.

3. Spoon shrimp and sauce over pasta. Sprinkle with remaining cilantro. Makes 8 servings.

Brands may vary by region; substitute a similar product.

PACIFIC SEAFOOD
Northwest Cioppino ▼

1/4 cup extra-virgin olive oil
1 cup chopped shallots
6 garlic cloves, minced
3 celery ribs, chopped
1 large yellow onion, chopped
1 green bell pepper, sliced in 2-inch julienne strips
2 red bell peppers, sliced in 2-inch julienne strips
1 medium orange, both grated peel and juice
1 teaspoon red pepper flakes (or more to taste)
1 cup white dry vermouth
2 cups fish or chicken stock
1 6-ounce can tomato paste

1 28-ounce can tomatoes, chopped with juice
1/2 cup chopped fresh parsley
1 teaspoon dried basil
1 teaspoon dried oregano
1 teaspoon dried thyme
1 teaspoon crumbled saffron threads
1 bay leaf
2 pounds golden clams, well washed
2 pounds black mussels, well washed
1 pound prawns (U/15), peeled, deveined, with tails left on
3 Dungeness crabs, cooked, cleaned and broken in half
2 pounds halibut fillet (or cod), cut in 1 1/2-inch cubes

1. In a large, heavy stockpot, combine olive oil, shallots, garlic, celery and onion. Sauté over medium heat, stirring frequently, until onion is translucent and tender, 5-6 minutes. Do not brown.

2. Add bell peppers and sauté for 5-6 minutes, stirring frequently.

3. Add all remaining ingredients except seafood. Bring to a boil. Reduce heat to a light simmer and cook for 20 minutes, stirring occasionally.

4. Add clams and mussels. Simmer for 4 minutes.

5. Add prawns, crabs and halibut. Simmer for 5-6 minutes, or until prawns are opaque.

6. Divide seafood equally into 6 large soup bowls. Top with broth and serve with French/sourdough bread and butter. Makes 6 servings.

PacificSeafood™

Entrées

Sunkist

SUNKIST
Citrus Scampi ◀

20 large raw shrimp (about 1 pound), peeled,
   deveined, tails on
4 tablespoons butter
4 tablespoons olive oil
2 teaspoons minced garlic
12 Sunkist* fresh orange segments
12 Sunkist* fresh lemon segments
12 Sunkist* fresh grapefruit segments
8 cups baby spinach leaves

1. Butterfly the shrimp, slicing down the back and almost in half.
This will make the shrimp curl when cooking.
2. Melt butter with the olive oil in a large skillet over medium heat.
Stir in garlic and shrimp. Cook shrimp for 4-5 minutes, or until they
turn pink and their tails curl; remove from pan.
3. Add orange, lemon and grapefruit segments to the pan;
stir gently to heat through.
4. Place 2 cups baby spinach leaves on each serving plate. Arrange
the shrimp on top of the spinach. Pour the citrus segments over
the shrimp. Serve immediately. Makes 4 servings.

Tip: This can also be served over rice.

Brands may vary by region; substitute a similar product.

JOHNNY'S
Sautéed Garlic Prawns ▲

1-2 pounds prawns, peeled and deveined
1 1/2 tablespoons Johnny's* Great Caesar Garlic Spread and Seasoning
1 tablespoon lemon juice
1/2 teaspoon black pepper, optional
1 tablespoon white wine, optional
1/2 cup butter or margarine

1. Combine prawns with Johnny's Garlic Spread, lemon juice, pepper and
wine in a glass bowl. Cover and refrigerate for 1 hour.
2. Melt butter in a large nonstick pan over medium-high heat. Transfer the
prawns to the hot pan and cook for 2 minutes on each side, or until bright
pink and opaque.
3. Serve prawns over rice or pasta. Makes 2-4 servings.

Brands may vary by region; substitute a similar product.

Johnny's

SeaPak
Fresh Artichokes Farci with Shrimp and Sherry ▲

4 large fresh artichokes
8 ounces unsalted butter
12 ounces SeaPak Shrimp Scampi
1 teaspoon finely chopped garlic
1/4 cup pitted, chopped black olives
1 teaspoon chopped Italian parsley
1 1/2 cups bread crumbs, unseasoned
1/4 cup dry sherry
Salt, pepper and red pepper flakes
1/4 cup grated Parmesan cheese
Lemon wedges or garlic oil

1. Preheat oven to 325°F.
2. Steam artichokes in salted water until centers are tender; rinse under cold water, drain and let cool.
3. Melt butter in a large sauté pan over medium heat. Add shrimp, garlic, olives, parsley, bread crumbs, sherry, and salt, pepper and red pepper flakes to taste. Cook until shrimp are tender; remove pan from heat and let cool.
4. Clean artichokes by removing the choke and trimming the leaves. Fill each artichoke to the top with the shrimp filling.
5. Top with grated Parmesan and bake until heated through. Serve hot with lemon wedges or garlic oil. Makes 4 servings.

ATLANTIC CAPES
Scallop and Leek Stir-Fry with Pine Nuts ◄

1 ¹/₂ **pounds U/10 Atlantic Capes* sea scallops**
2 **tablespoons vegetable oil**
4 **leeks (white part only),**
    cleaned and cut in thin strips or rings
2 **teaspoons grated fresh ginger**
3 **garlic cloves, minced**
¹/₄ **cup sherry**
¹/₄ **cup tamari or soy sauce**
1 **teaspoon toasted sesame oil**
3 **tablespoons toasted pine nuts**
Red pepper flakes, optional

1. If scallops are frozen, thaw in the refrigerator for
3 hours or overnight.
2. Heat oil in a large sauté pan over medium-high heat. Sauté leeks
until soft. Add ginger and garlic and cook
for another 2 minutes, taking care to not burn the garlic.
Add scallops and sauté until opaque.
3. Add sherry and tamari to the pan and bring to a boil. Lower the
heat and cook for 1 minute.
4. Remove the pan from the heat and stir in sesame oil, pine nuts
and red pepper flakes to taste. Serve over rice
or pasta. Makes 4-6 servings.

* Brands may vary by region; substitute a similar product.

143

Entrées

KIRKLAND SIGNATURE
Pan-Seared Scallops and Citrus Saffron Beurre Blanc

1 pound Kirkland Signature scallops, defrosted
Salt and pepper
1 tablespoon olive oil

CITRUS SAFFRON BEURRE BLANC
1 cup Chardonnay
2 tablespoons minced garlic
2 tablespoons lemon juice
Pinch of saffron
6 ounces heavy cream
4 ounces unsalted butter, cut into small pieces

1. To make Beurre Blanc, combine wine, garlic, lemon juice and saffron in a stainless-steel saucepan. Bring to a simmer and reduce by half. Add cream and reduce by half. Turn the heat to high and whisk in cut-up butter, 2-3 pieces at a time, until all butter is well incorporated. Finish with a handheld mixer.
2. Season scallops to taste with salt and pepper. Heat olive oil in a sauté pan over medium-high heat. Brown scallops until opaque in the center.
3. Place scallops on plates and top with sauce. Makes 4 servings.

KIRKLAND SIGNATURE
Scallops with Red Peppers and Snow Peas

8 ounces linguine
1 tablespoon olive oil
3 garlic cloves
1 tablespoon cornstarch
2 tablespoons cold water
1/2 cup dry white wine
1 teaspoon black pepper
1 pound Kirkland Signature scallops, defrosted
1/4 cup grated Parmesan cheese
1/2 cup julienned red bell pepper
1/2 cup snow peas
1/4 cup chopped parsley

1. Cook linguine according to package directions, without adding oil or salt. Drain.
2. Meanwhile, in a large skillet or wok, heat olive oil over medium heat. Sauté garlic until golden, but do not burn.
3. In a small bowl, mix cornstarch and cold water until smooth. Add cornstarch mixture, wine and black pepper to the skillet; bring to a boil.
4. Add scallops and Parmesan; simmer for 1-2 minutes. Add pepper strips and snow peas; simmer 1-2 minutes, stirring gently. Remove garlic.
5. Toss linguine with hot scallops. Sprinkle with parsley. Makes 4 servings.

AMERICAN PRIDE SEAFOODS
Garlic Rosemary Scallop Kabobs ▼

2 pounds American Pride* U/10 frozen scallops

2 red bell peppers, cut in 1-inch squares

1/2 cup olive oil

1 tablespoon rosemary, crushed with a spoon to
   bring out flavor and make smaller pieces

3 garlic cloves, finely minced, or 1 tablespoon garlic powder

1 teaspoon kosher salt

Black pepper

1. Thaw scallops overnight in the refrigerator.

2. Marinate scallops and peppers in olive oil, rosemary, garlic, salt and black pepper to taste for 30 minutes.

3. Preheat grill.

4. Thread peppers and scallops alternately onto skewers, using 4 scallops per skewer.

5. Cook on a very hot grill for 2 1/2 minutes per side, or until scallops are done. Makes 5 servings.

* Brands may vary by region; substitute a similar product.

NATURESWEET
Grape Tomatoes with Penne and Scallops

12 ounces penne pasta
2 tablespoons olive oil
3 cups thinly sliced mushrooms
2 garlic cloves, minced
1 pound NatureSweet* grape tomatoes
1 pound bay scallops
1 teaspoon salt
1/2 teaspoon ground pepper
1/4 teaspoon red pepper flakes
1/4 cup coarsely chopped fresh basil
Parsley sprigs

1. Cook pasta until al dente in a large pot of boiling water, stirring occasionally. Drain.
2. Heat oil in a skillet over medium heat. Add mushrooms, garlic and 12 ounces tomatoes. Sauté for 5 minutes.
3. Add scallops and sauté for another 2 minutes, or until just cooked through. Season with salt and pepper.
4. Remove from heat; add red pepper flakes, basil and pasta to the skillet and toss.
5. Cut remaining tomatoes in half. Garnish each serving with tomatoes and parsley sprigs. Makes 4-6 servings.

Brands may vary by region; substitute a similar product.

PHILLIPS
Lemon Caper Crab Cakes ▲

4 tablespoons butter, divided
2 tablespoons minced yellow onion
2 large eggs
2 tablespoons lemon juice
1 tablespoon capers, drained
2 tablespoons mayonnaise
1/4 teaspoon garlic powder
1/2 teaspoon lemon pepper seasoning
1 teaspoon Worcestershire sauce
1/4 teaspoon salt
2/3 cup plain bread crumbs, lightly toasted
1 pound Phillips* Crab Meat

1. Melt 2 tablespoons butter in a medium sauté pan over medium heat. Cook onion until soft; set aside to cool.
2. In a medium bowl, beat eggs until frothy. Stir in cooked onion, lemon juice, capers, mayonnaise, garlic powder, lemon pepper seasoning, Worcestershire sauce and salt until well blended. Fold in bread crumbs, then crab.
3. Form 8 round cakes, using approximately 1/2 cup of mixture for each.
4. Heat remaining butter in a sauté pan over medium-low heat. Cook crab cakes until golden brown, about 2-3 minutes per side. Makes 4 servings.

Brands may vary by region; substitute a similar product.

DELTA PRIDE
Parmesan Catfish ▼

2 tablespoons margarine, melted
1/2 cup grated Parmesan cheese
1/4 cup yellow cornmeal
1/4 cup flour
1/2 teaspoon pepper
1 teaspoon paprika
2 pounds Delta Pride catfish fillets

1. Preheat oven to 400°F. Pour melted margarine into a large baking pan.

2. Combine Parmesan, cornmeal, flour, pepper and paprika in a paper bag or zipper-lock bag. Place catfish in the bag and shake to coat each fillet.

3. Place fish in the pan, turning once to coat with margarine. Sprinkle remaining cheese/cornmeal mixture over fish.

4. Bake for 10-15 minutes, or until golden brown and fish flakes when tested with a fork. Makes 8 servings.

CLEAR SPRINGS
Rainbow Trout in Parchment ▲

2 tablespoons chopped parsley
1 tablespoon olive oil
1/2 tablespoon minced garlic
1/2 tablespoon minced orange peel
1/8 teaspoon salt
1/8 teaspoon black pepper
2 pieces parchment paper, 15 by 15 inches
2 1-pound dressed Clear Springs* rainbow trout

1. Preheat oven to 375°F. Combine parsley, olive oil, garlic, orange peel, salt and pepper in a small bowl.

2. Fold each piece of parchment in half. Open and place each trout, skin side down, with the back close to the fold. Evenly spread 2 teaspoons of filling on the flesh side of the bottom half of trout. Fold trout closed. Bring top half of parchment over trout and fold edges together to form a tight seal.

3. Place parchment packages on a baking sheet; bake for 12-15 minutes. Makes 2 servings.

Tip: Packets can be prepared ahead and refrigerated, tightly covered, for up to 4 hours.

* Brands may vary by region; substitute a similar product.

WESTERN UNITED FISH COMPANY
Seared Ahi Tuna Steaks ▲

5 garlic cloves, finely chopped
1/2 cup soy sauce
Juice of 2 lemons
1/2 teaspoon freshly ground black pepper
Pinch of salt
Dash of sesame oil
2 fresh Western United Fish Company ahi tuna steaks,
    1 1/2 inches thick
Canola oil

1. Preheat grill.

2. In a bowl, whisk together garlic, soy sauce, lemon juice, pepper, salt and sesame oil. Place ahi steaks in a glass dish. Pour marinade over steaks, turn to coat, cover and refrigerate for 10 minutes.

3. Brush grill with canola oil. Grill ahi steaks over direct high heat for 2 minutes per side, or until cooked to your taste. Serve immediately with steamed vegetables and rice. Makes 2 servings.

Western United Fish Company
Your Direct Source

GOLD-N-SOFT
Halibut with Hazelnut Crust ▼

2 cups ground hazelnuts
1 cup dried bread crumbs
1/4 cup Gold-N-Soft* Margarine, melted
2 tablespoons dried savory
4 5-ounce halibut fillets (or other lean white fish fillets)
2 cups heavy cream
1/2 cup freshly grated Parmesan cheese
1 lemon, cut in wedges

1. Preheat oven to 450°F.
2. Combine hazelnuts, bread crumbs, margarine and savory in a bowl; mix until well blended. Roll and press halibut into hazelnut mixture.
3. Place fillets on a greased broiling pan and bake for 8-10 minutes, or until just cooked through.
4. Meanwhile, pour cream into a nonreactive saucepan and cook over medium-high heat to reduce volume by half. Add Parmesan to cream; mix well.
5. Place fish on a serving platter and top with sauce. Serve with lemon wedges. Makes 4 servings.

Brands may vary by region; substitute a similar product.

Ventura Foods,LLC

Easy Cooking The Costco Way

WILSONBATIZ
Fillets of Sole with Grapes and Walnuts ▲

1/2 cup veal stock

8 fillets of sole

Salt and pepper

Vegetable oil

24 WilsonBatiz* grapes (white muscat, red globe
    or other variety), peeled and seeded

16 walnut halves

Juice of 1 lemon

1 teaspoon chopped parsley

1. Heat veal stock in a small saucepan and keep warm.

2. Season fillets with salt and pepper to taste. Sauté in oil over medium-high heat for 2-3 minutes per side; remove from the pan and keep warm.

3. Add grapes and walnuts to the pan and sauté briefly.

4. Arrange sole on a serving dish. Cover with grapes and walnuts.

5. Stir lemon juice into the hot veal stock and warm briefly; pour around the sole. Garnish with parsley. Makes 8 servings.

Brands may vary by region; substitute a similar product.

ORCA BAY
Grilled Mahi Mahi with Tangy Cilantro Sauce ▲

1/2 cup honey

1/2 cup water

1/4 cup rice vinegar

1/4 cup white wine

1 tablespoon cornstarch

1 teaspoon granulated garlic

1/2 teaspoon grated lemon peel

2 tablespoons chopped fresh cilantro,
    plus more for garnish

2 pounds Orca Bay* frozen
    mahi mahi fillets, thawed

1. Preheat grill.

2. Combine honey, water, vinegar, wine, cornstarch, garlic and lemon peel in a small saucepan. Cook, stirring, over medium heat until mixture boils and thickens; lower heat and simmer for 2 minutes. Stir in cilantro. Remove sauce from heat and keep warm.

3. Grill fish 4-6 inches from the heat for 10 minutes per inch of thickness, or until it turns opaque and flakes easily with a fork. (Mahi mahi can also be baked in a 300°F oven for 20 minutes.)

4. Spoon sauce over fish and garnish with cilantro. Makes 4 servings.

Tip: Thaw mahi mahi in the refrigerator for 6-8 hours or overnight, or in the microwave on low for up to 2 minutes, checking every 30 seconds.

Brands may vary by region; substitute a similar product.

MOUNTAIN STREAM TILAPIA
Tilapia in Lemon Sauce with Capers ▲

2 tablespoons oil
Flour for coating
4 6-ounce Mountain Stream* tilapia fillets
1/4 cup diced onions
1/2 cup unsalted butter
1 1/2 tablespoons capers
1/2 cup white wine
1/2 cup lemon juice
Salt and pepper
1/2 bunch parsley, finely chopped

1. Heat oil in a very large pan over high heat (or cook in 2 batches). Lightly flour tilapia fillets and sear until golden brown, 3-4 minutes.
2. Turn fillets and add onions. Cook briefly until onions are translucent; add butter, capers, wine, lemon juice, and salt and pepper to taste.
3. Reduce heat to medium and simmer for about 5 minutes. When the sauce has a silky consistency, add parsley.
4. Serve with baked potatoes. Makes 4 servings.

Brands may vary by region; substitute a similar product.

RIO MAR
Tilapia Fillets en Papillote ▲

2 carrots, peeled and julienned
2 zucchini, julienned
4 teaspoons minced fresh ginger
2 tablespoons minced fresh basil
4 tablespoons olive oil
4 tablespoons lime juice
4 tablespoons white wine
Salt and pepper to taste
1 pound fresh Rio Mar* tilapia fillets

1. Preheat oven to 400°F.
2. Layer ingredients in the order listed on 4 separate 6-by-10-inch pieces of aluminum foil. Close the foil to make 4 sealed "pouches."
3. Bake until fish is tender, 15-20 minutes. Open the pouches and serve tilapia on a bed of steamed vegetables. (Caution: when pouches are opened, escaping steam can cause burns.) Makes 4 servings.

Brands may vary by region; substitute a similar product.

RAIN FOREST AQUACULTURE
Rollatini of Tilapia Surprise ▲

2 fresh Rain Forest* tilapia fillets
4 large shrimp
1 ounce fresh snow crab meat
$1/2$ ounce sun-dried tomatoes, chopped
Salt and pepper
1 cup flour
4 eggs, beaten
2 cups bread crumbs
2 teaspoons butter
2 small shallots, diced
1 pint whipping cream
1 cup finely chopped tomatoes
Madeira

1. Preheat oven to 325°F.
2. Pound tilapia fillets until flat. Layer the shrimp, crab and sun-dried tomatoes on the fillets. Season to taste with salt and pepper. Roll up the fillets and secure with toothpicks. Dip in flour, dip in eggs and then roll in bread crumbs.
3. Deep-fry until golden brown. Transfer to the oven and bake for 10 minutes.
4. Melt butter in a sauté pan and sweat shallots until tender. Stir in cream and tomatoes; heat gently, then add a splash of Madeira.
5. Slice rollatini and serve with sauce. Makes 2 servings.

Brands may vary by region; substitute a similar product.

REGAL SPRINGS
Tilapia in White Vermouth Sauce ▲

$3/4$ cup dry vermouth
$3/4$ cup water
4 thin strips lemon peel
2 teaspoons small capers with juice
1 tablespoon finely chopped shallots
$1/2$ teaspoon minced garlic
4 Regal Springs* tilapia fillets
Lemon wedges

1. In a large sauté pan, combine vermouth and water; heat until it just begins to bubble. Stir in lemon peel, capers with juice, shallots and garlic.
2. Add tilapia to the pan and cook over medium heat for 3-4 minutes; turn fillets with a large spatula and cook 3-4 minutes, or until just cooked through. Turn the fillets again and warm for 30 seconds; remove to plates and top with sauce.
3. Serve with lemon wedges and spicy rice or fettuccine Alfredo.
Makes 4 servings.

Brands may vary by region; substitute a similar product.

HIGH LINER
Pan-Fried Tilapia with Toasted Head Roasted Pineapple-Avocado Salsa ▼

1/2 cup lime juice
4 High Liner* tilapia
   loins, thawed
1/2 cup flour
1 1/2 teaspoons chili powder
1 teaspoon ground cumin
1 teaspoon sea salt
1/2 teaspoon black pepper
Pinch of cayenne pepper
2 eggs, beaten
1/4 cup cooking oil

TOASTED HEAD ROASTED PINEAPPLE-AVOCADO SALSA

1 cup diced fresh pineapple
1/2 jalapeño pepper, minced
1/3 cup Toasted Head Chardonnay
1 tomato, cut in small dice
1/2 small red onion, cut in small dice
1/4 cup cilantro, chopped
1 pickled jalapeño pepper, minced
Juice of 1/2 lemon
1 1/2 teaspoons salt
1 avocado, cut in small dice

1. Pour lime juice over tilapia, cover and refrigerate. Combine flour and spices.

2. To make the salsa, place a nonstick skillet over medium-high heat; add pineapple and fresh jalapeño. Cook for 4 minutes, stirring to brown evenly. Add wine and cook for 1 minute; transfer to a bowl. Add remaining ingredients and toss gently; cover and refrigerate.

3. Dip tilapia in egg, then in seasoned flour. Heat oil in a large nonstick skillet over medium-high heat. Add tilapia and cook about 4 1/2 minutes; turn and cook 4 1/2 minutes. Remove and top with salsa. Makes 4 servings.

Recipe created by Rachael Levine, Executive Winery Chef, R. H. Phillips Winery.
* Brands may vary by region; substitute a similar product.

Desserts

COLUMBIA MARKETING INTERNATIONAL
Caramel-Glazed Apple Cake ◄

CAKE
1 cup packed light brown sugar
1 cup granulated sugar
1 1/2 cups vegetable oil
3 eggs
3 cups all-purpose flour
1 teaspoon baking soda
2 teaspoons cinnamon
1/2 teaspoon nutmeg
1/2 teaspoon salt
5 Washington Granny Smith
   or Golden Delicious apples,
   cored, peeled and cut in
   1/2-inch pieces
1 1/4 cups chopped pecans
   or walnuts
2 1/4 teaspoons vanilla extract

CARAMEL GLAZE
4 tablespoons butter
1/4 cup granulated sugar
1/4 cup light brown sugar
Pinch of salt
1/2 cup heavy cream

1. Preheat oven to 325°F. Butter and flour a 9-by-13-inch pan.
2. To prepare the cake, beat both sugars and oil in a mixing bowl until very well blended. Add eggs one at a time, beating well after each addition. Sift together flour, baking soda, cinnamon, nutmeg and salt; gradually add to eggs, mixing just until blended. Stir in apples, pecans and vanilla; pour into pan.
3. Bake for 50-75 minutes, or until a toothpick inserted in the center comes out clean. Let cool in the pan while preparing the glaze.
4. To prepare the glaze, melt butter in a saucepan over low heat. Stir in both sugars and salt; cook over medium-low heat for 2 minutes. Add cream and boil for 2 minutes, stirring constantly.
5. Poke holes in the cake with a skewer or toothpick. Pour on the glaze. Serve warm or at room temperature. Top with whipped cream or ice cream if desired. Makes 12 servings.

CHELAN FRUIT
Apple Cake ▲

2 teaspoons vanilla extract
2 cups sugar
1/2 cup butter, softened
2 eggs
2 cups flour
2 teaspoons baking soda
2 teaspoons cinnamon
1/2 teaspoon salt
1/2 teaspoon nutmeg
4 cups peeled, chopped Trout* Crisp Granny Smith apples
1 cup chopped nuts
1 cup raisins

1. Preheat oven to 350°F.
2. Cream together vanilla, sugar, butter and eggs in a large bowl.
3. Sift together flour, baking soda, cinnamon, salt and nutmeg in a medium bowl; add to butter mixture.
4. Stir in apples, nuts and raisins. Pour mixture into an ungreased 9-by-13-inch pan.
5. Bake for 45-50 minutes, or until a toothpick inserted in the center comes out clean. Makes 12 servings.

Brands may vary by region; substitute a similar product.

NONNI'S
Upside-Down Peach Cioccolati Cake ▲

2 tablespoons butter, melted

1/4 cup brown sugar

3-4 fresh, firm peaches, thinly sliced

2 Nonni's* Cioccolati Biscotti, chopped in large chunks, plus 1 cup ground Nonni's Cioccolati Biscotti (use food processor or blender)

1 4.6-ounce box French vanilla instant pudding

2 eggs

1/4 cup real sour cream

1/2 cup canned sweetened condensed milk

1/2 teaspoon vanilla extract

1. Preheat oven to 350°F. Mix butter and brown sugar; spread in a greased 6-inch round baking pan.

2. Arrange peaches on the butter/sugar mixture. Sprinkle biscotti chunks over peaches.

3. On medium-low speed, blend pudding, eggs, sour cream, condensed milk, vanilla and ground biscotti until thoroughly mixed (1-2 minutes). Batter may be gritty. Pour over the crumbled biscotti. Batter may reach the top of the pan.

4. Bake, attentively, for 40-50 minutes, or until center is golden brown. Cake may rise above the top of the pan during baking. Let cool, then invert pan onto a serving dish. Makes 4-6 servings.

Tip: Recipe can be doubled, using a 9-by-13-inch pan or a 12-inch round pan.

Brands may vary by region; substitute a similar product.

L&M
Grandma Mary's Apple Cake ▲

1 1/2 cups sugar

1/2 cup vegetable oil

2 large eggs

2 cups unbleached white flour

1 teaspoon baking soda

1 teaspoon baking powder

1/2 teaspoon salt

1 teaspoon ground cinnamon

1/2 teaspoon ground nutmeg

1/2 teaspoon ground cloves

3 cups peeled, sliced Washington apples (any combination of L&M* Braeburn, Fuji, Gala or Red Delicious)

1 cup chopped pecans or walnuts

1. Preheat oven to 350°F.

2. Combine all ingredients in a large bowl. Mix with a wooden spoon until combined; dough will be very stiff. Spread in a buttered 9-by-13-inch pan.

3. Bake for 35 minutes, or until a toothpick inserted in the center comes out clean. This is excellent for picnics; it keeps well and stays moist. Makes 12 servings.

This recipe was submitted by Stephanie LaFollette, an L&M sales-support specialist in Selah, Washington.
* Brands may vary by region; substitute a similar product.

156

HELLMANN'S/BEST FOODS
Super Moist Chocolate Mayo Cake ▲

1 box (18 ¹/₄ ounces) chocolate cake mix
1 cup Hellmann's or Best Foods Real Mayonnaise
1 cup water
3 eggs
1 teaspoon ground cinnamon, optional

1. Preheat oven to 350°F. Spray and lightly flour two 9-inch round cake pans; set aside.
2. In a large bowl, with a mixer at low speed, blend cake mix, mayonnaise, water, eggs and cinnamon for 30 seconds. Beat at medium speed for 2 minutes. Pour into the prepared pans.
3. Bake for 30 minutes, or until the cake springs back when touched lightly in the center. Cool on a wire rack for 10 minutes; remove the cake from the pans and cool completely. Sprinkle, if desired, with confectioners' sugar or fill and frost. Makes 12 servings.

DOVEX MARKETING
Chocolate Pear Delight ▲

1 tablespoon butter
1 tablespoon flour
¹/₂ cup milk
3 tablespoons cocoa
2 ¹/₂ tablespoons sugar
2 eggs, separated
1 fresh Dovex Marketing* Northwest Anjou or Bosc pear, peeled and sliced

1. Preheat oven to 350°F.
2. Melt butter over medium-low heat in a small saucepan; blend in flour. In a separate pan, combine milk, cocoa and sugar and heat until hot but not boiling; add immediately to flour mixture, stirring constantly.
3. Beat egg yolks in a bowl until light. Blend a small amount of the hot sauce into the yolks; stir yolks into the sauce. Cook, stirring, over low heat until slightly thickened. Cover and cool.
4. Beat egg whites until stiff but not dry; fold into cooled chocolate mixture.
5. Lay sliced pears in a buttered 4-cup baking dish; pour chocolate mixture over pears. Bake for 30 minutes, or until set. Serve immediately. Makes 2 servings.

Tip: This recipe can be doubled for 4 servings.

Brands may vary by region; substitute a similar product.

Desserts I

STEMILT GROWERS
Apple Crisp ▼

1/3 cup sifted all-purpose flour

1/2 cup packed brown sugar

2 teaspoons ground cinnamon, divided

1/2 cup butter, melted

1 cup rolled oats or unsweetened granola

1/2 teaspoon salt

1/2 teaspoon ground nutmeg

6 large Stemilt* Pink Lady or Braeburn apples, peeled and chopped

1/2 cup granulated sugar

1. Preheat oven to 375°F. Lightly coat a 9-by-9-inch pan with nonstick cooking spray.

2. In a medium bowl, combine flour, brown sugar, 1 teaspoon cinnamon, butter, rolled oats, salt and nutmeg.

3. In a large bowl, combine apples, granulated sugar and 1 teaspoon cinnamon; pour into the baking pan. Cover evenly with topping, pressing it firmly onto apples.

4. Bake for 35 minutes, or until lightly browned. Serve warm with whipped topping or ice cream. Makes 6-8 servings.

* Brands may vary by region; substitute a similar product.

MOUNTAIN VIEW FRUIT SALES
Peach Cobbler ▲

1 stick (¹/₂ cup) butter or margarine
8 cups peeled and sliced I.M. Ripe label
   California peaches
2 cups sugar, divided
¹/₂ cup water
1 cup flour
2 teaspoons baking powder
³/₄ cup milk
Cinnamon

1. Preheat oven to 350°F. Melt butter in a 9-by-13-inch pan in the oven.
2. Combine peaches, 1 cup sugar and water in a large saucepan; heat just to a boil.
3. Combine flour, 1 cup sugar and baking powder in a medium bowl; stir in milk.
4. Pour batter over melted butter in the baking pan. Spoon fruit and juice over the batter. Sprinkle lightly with cinnamon. Bake for 35-40 minutes, or until golden brown. Makes 12 servings.

KINGSBURG APPLE
Phyllo Cups with Asian Pears and Pluots ▲

4 Kingsburg Apple pluots
2 Kingsburg Apple Asian pears
1-1 ¹/₄ cups sugar (to taste)
1 ¹/₂ teaspoons ground cinnamon
¹/₂ teaspoon ground ginger
¹/₂ cup chopped walnuts
1 pound prepared phyllo dough
4 ounces butter (¹/₂ cup), melted
Whipped cream or ice cream

1. Preheat oven to 375°F. Butter 8-10 cups of a muffin tin.
2. Cut pluots and Asian pears in ¹/₂-inch cubes; place in a bowl. Toss with ¹/₂ cup sugar, cinnamon, ginger and walnuts. Set aside.
3. Layer 8 sheets of phyllo, brushing each layer with melted butter and sprinkling with about 2 teaspoons sugar. Cut layered phyllo dough into 6-inch rounds. Place the phyllo rounds in the muffin cups and press to fit. Fill with the fruit mixture.
4. Bake for 20-25 minutes, or until golden brown. Serve immediately, topped with whipped cream or ice cream. Makes 8-10 servings.

Kingsburg Apple Sales

Desserts I

EQUAL
Country Peach Tart ▲

Pastry dough for single-crust 9-inch pie

4 cups peeled, sliced fresh peaches or
    frozen peaches, thawed

12 packets Equal sweetener
    (or $^1/_2$ cup Equal Spoonful or Equal Sugar Lite)

1 tablespoon all-purpose flour

$^1/_2$ teaspoon ground cinnamon

$^1/_4$ teaspoon almond extract

1. Preheat oven to 425°F.
2. Roll out pastry dough on a floured surface into a 12-inch circle;
transfer to an ungreased baking sheet. In a bowl, combine peaches, Equal,
flour, cinnamon and almond extract; toss until peaches are coated.
3. Arrange peaches on pastry, leaving a 2-inch border around the edges.
Bring pastry edges toward the center, overlapping as necessary.
4. Bake for 25-30 minutes, or until the crust is golden brown and the
peaches are tender. Serve warm or at room temperature. Makes 8 servings.

WESTERN SWEET CHERRY
Handmade Stem-Free
Cherry Almond Pie ▲

Pastry dough for 2-crust 9-inch pie

$^1/_2$ cup finely chopped almonds, divided

1 egg, beaten

4 cups pitted stem-free Northwest*
    fresh sweet cherries

$^1/_3$ cup sugar

3 tablespoons cornstarch

1 teaspoon ground cinnamon

$^1/_4$ teaspoon salt

2 tablespoons red wine

1. Preheat oven to 375°F.
2. Roll dough into a 16-inch circle and sprinkle with $^1/_4$ cup almonds;
roll gently to embed nuts in dough. Gently transfer to a lightly greased
baking sheet lined with parchment paper. Brush with beaten egg.
3. Mix cherries, sugar, cornstarch, cinnamon, salt and wine in a bowl; spoon
onto dough, leaving a 4-inch border. Lift edges of dough up and over fruit,
leaving a 5-inch circle of cherries showing in the center.
Fold in edges of pastry to form a circle. Brush pastry with egg; sprinkle with
remaining almonds.
4. Bake for 30 minutes, or until pastry browns and filling bubbles.
Let stand 15 minutes before cutting. Makes 8 servings.

Brands may vary by region; substitute a similar product.

GROWER DIRECT/PRIMAVERA/M&R
Cherry Crème Cheese Pie ▲

3 cups pitted Bing cherries, about 2 pounds

1 ¹/₂ cups sugar, divided

1 ¹/₂-2 tablespoons cornstarch

1 package graham crackers, crushed

¹/₄ cup margarine, melted

1 3-ounce package cream cheese, softened

¹/₂ cup confectioners' sugar

¹/₂ teaspoon vanilla extract

¹/₂ pint whipping cream

1. Combine cherries and 1 cup sugar in a saucepan; cook over low heat until cherries are soft, 20-30 minutes. Mix cornstarch with ¹/₄ cup sugar in a small bowl; stir in ¹/₂ cup of cooled cooking juice. Stir into cherries and cook until thickened. Let cool.

2. Combine graham cracker crumbs, margarine and ¹/₄ cup sugar; pat into a 9-inch pie pan. Put in the freezer while making the filling.

3. Place cream cheese, confectioners' sugar and vanilla in a mixing bowl and beat until smooth. In another bowl, whip the cream until soft peaks form; fold into cream cheese mixture. Pour into the crust.

4. Top with the cooled cherries and refrigerate for 5 hours or overnight before serving. Makes 6-8 servings.

GROWER DIRECT/PRIMAVERA/M&R
Michael's Killer Cobbler ▲

1 ¹/₄ cups Grower Direct* blueberries

1 ¹/₄ cups Bing cherries, halved and pitted

1 ³/₄ cups sugar, divided

³/₄ cup warm water

6 tablespoons butter

1 cup all-purpose flour

1 teaspoon baking powder

1 cup milk

1. Preheat oven to 350°F.

2. Place blueberries, cherries, ³/₄ cup sugar and water in a bowl and stir to combine.

3. Melt butter in a large ovenproof baking dish, swirling to coat the bottom.

4. In a separate bowl, combine flour, 1 cup sugar, baking powder and milk; mix well. Pour into the baking dish. Spread fruit mixture with liquid evenly over the batter.

5. Bake for 1 hour, or until crust is done. Serve warm with vanilla ice cream. Makes 6-8 servings.

* Brands may vary by region; substitute a similar product.

Desserts |

QUAKER
Easy Apple-Berry Crumble Pie ▼

1 1/2 cups Quaker Oats (quick or old-fashioned), uncooked
1 cup all-purpose flour
1/2 cup firmly packed brown sugar
1/2 teaspoon baking soda
10 tablespoons butter or margarine, melted
1 21-ounce can apple pie filling
3/4 cup sweetened dried cranberries
1 1/2 teaspoons lemon juice
1/2 teaspoon ground cinnamon

1. Preheat oven to 375°F. Lightly coat an 8- or 9-inch glass pie pan with nonstick cooking spray.

2. In a medium bowl, combine oats, flour, brown sugar and baking soda. Add melted butter; mix well. Set aside 3/4 cup of the oat mixture for topping. Press the remaining oat mixture firmly onto the bottom and sides of the pie pan. Bake for 10-12 minutes, or until light golden brown. Cool slightly on a wire rack.

3. Using the same bowl, stir together pie filling, cranberries, lemon juice and cinnamon. Spoon the filling over the hot crust, spreading evenly. Sprinkle evenly with the reserved oat topping.

4. Bake for 18-22 minutes, or until the topping is golden brown. Serve warm or at room temperature. Makes 8 servings.

ALL STATE PACKERS/ ASSOCIATED FRUIT
Pear Praline Pie ▲

PRALINE TOPPING
1/2 cup packed brown sugar
1/2 cup chopped pecans
1/3 cup flour
1/4 cup butter

5 fresh ripe Green Bartlett or Bosc pears
2/3 cup sugar
1/4 cup flour
1/2 teaspoon grated lemon peel
1/2 teaspoon ground ginger
Dash of salt
1 unbaked 9-inch pie shell

1. Preheat oven to 400°F.
2. Prepare Praline Topping: In a medium bowl, combine brown sugar, pecans and flour. Cut in butter.
3. Peel, core and slice pears. Place in a large bowl and toss with sugar, flour, lemon peel, ginger and salt.
4. Sprinkle 1/4 of topping in pie shell. Add pears. Sprinkle with remaining topping. Bake for 40 minutes, or until golden brown. Serve warm or cold. Top with whipped cream or ice cream, if desired. Makes 6-8 servings.
Tip: Always be sure to use ripe pears.

SAGE FRUIT COMPANY
Julie's Jonagold Apple Pie ▲

Pastry dough for 2-crust 9-inch pie
5-7 medium to large Sage Fruit Company* Jonagold apples, peeled, cored and sliced
3/4 cup sugar
1/3 cup flour
1/2 teaspoon cinnamon
(careful—too much will overpower the apples!)

1. Preheat oven to 425°F. Roll out half of pastry dough and place in a 9-inch pie pan.
2. In a large bowl, combine apples, sugar, flour and cinnamon; pour into the pie shell. Moisten outer edge of crust with water. Roll out remaining dough and place on top of pie; crimp the edges to seal. Make several slits in the top crust.
3. Bake on the lowest oven rack for 40-45 minutes, or until the crust is brown and the juices are bubbly. If necessary, cover the edges with strips of foil to prevent the crust from getting too dark. Serve cold or warm with vanilla ice cream. Makes 6-8 servings.

Brands may vary by region; substitute a similar product.

WESPAK
Tree-Ripe Plum Pie ▲

2 cups all-purpose flour
1 1/4 teaspoons salt, divided
2/3 cup + 2 tablespoons shortening
1/4 cup cold water
5 cups unpeeled sliced WesPak Friar plums
1/4 cup tapioca
1 cup sugar
1 teaspoon almond extract

1. Preheat oven to 425°F.
2. Combine flour and 1 teaspoon salt in a bowl. Cut in shortening until particles are the size of small peas. Mix in cold water with a fork. Roll out half of dough and line a 9-inch pie pan.
3. Place plums in a bowl and stir in tapioca, sugar, almond extract and 1/4 teaspoon salt. Pour into the pie shell.
4. Roll out remaining dough and place on top of filling. Crimp edges, slit top and sprinkle with sugar.
5. Bake for 15 minutes. Reduce heat to 325°F and bake for 40-50 minutes, or until crust is golden brown and filling is bubbling. Makes 6-8 servings.
Tips: Use any variety of ripe, flavorful plums. To enjoy year-round, slice plums and freeze for later use.

JON DONAIRE
Bananas Foster Cheesecake ▲

1 tablespoon chopped pecans
5 ounces Jon Donaire* Baked New York Cheesecake (1 precut slice)
1/2 ripe banana, peeled and cut in 1/4-inch slices
2 tablespoons purchased caramel sauce, warmed
Whipped cream
Cinnamon

1. Preheat oven to 350°F. Toast pecans on a baking sheet for 5-10 minutes, or until fragrant.
2. Place cheesecake slice on a dessert plate. Top with banana slices, letting them cascade down the sides.
3. Spoon warm caramel sauce carefully over cheesecake and banana slices. Sprinkle with toasted pecans.
4. Pipe a dollop of whipped cream onto back end of cake, then lightly sprinkle cake and plate with cinnamon. Makes 1 serving.
* Brands may vary by region; substitute a similar product.

RASKAS
Classic New York-Style Cheesecake ▲

8 zwieback toast slices, crushed
1 tablespoon butter, melted
1 tablespoon plus 1 1/3 cups sugar
4 eggs
2 teaspoons vanilla extract
4 8-ounce packages Raskas* cream cheese, softened
16 ounces sour cream
1/2 cup raisins, optional

1. Preheat oven to 325°F.
2. Mix zwieback crumbs, butter and 1 tablespoon sugar. Press into the bottom of a 10-inch springform pan.
3. Beat eggs in a medium bowl until thick and lemon colored, about 5 minutes. Add 1 1/3 cups sugar and vanilla. Set aside.
4. Beat cream cheese in a large bowl until smooth. Blend in egg mixture and sour cream. Pour into the pan. Sprinkle raisins over the top.
5. Bake for 1 hour. Turn the oven off and leave cake in the oven with the door ajar for 1 hour. Remove cake from the oven and let cool for 1 hour at room temperature. Chill. Makes 12-16 servings.

Brands may vary by region; substitute a similar product.

SCHREIBER™

THE CHEESECAKE FACTORY
Original Cheesecake
with Strawberries ▲

1 slice The Cheesecake Factory* Original Cheesecake
3 whole fresh strawberries
1 ounce prepared strawberry glaze
4 ounces whipped cream

1. Place cheesecake on a dessert plate.
2. Clean and remove stems from strawberries. Roll strawberries in strawberry glaze until lightly coated.
3. Garnish the cheesecake with the glazed strawberries.
4. Place whipped cream decoratively on the cheesecake and plate.
Makes 1 serving.

Brands may vary by region; substitute a similar product.

The Cheesecake Factory

Desserts

SMUCKER'S
Raspberry Twists

2 cups all-purpose flour
1 tablespoon baking powder
1/2 teaspoon salt
2 tablespoons sugar
1/2 cup Crisco* shortening
1/2 cup milk
1/2 cup Smucker's* Red Raspberry Preserves
    (or Strawberry or Apricot Preserves)
1/4 cup flaked coconut

1. Preheat oven to 450°F.

2. In a mixing bowl, combine flour, baking powder, salt and sugar.
Cut in Crisco shortening with a pastry blender or a fork until mixture
resembles coarse crumbs. Make a well in the center of the dry ingredients;
add milk all at once. Stir with a fork until the dough clings together.
Turn the dough onto a lightly floured surface; knead for 10-12 strokes.
Roll dough into an 8-by-15-inch rectangle.

3. Spread Smucker's preserves over the dough. Sprinkle with coconut.

4. Fold dough in half to make a 4-by-15-inch rectangle. Cut in 1-inch
strips. Holding strips at both ends, twist twice. Place on a lightly
greased baking sheet.

5. Bake for 10-12 minutes, or until golden brown. Makes 15 twists.

Brands may vary by region; substitute a similar product.

GENERAL MILLS BAKERIES & FOODSERVICE
Triple-Berry Cheesecake Croissant Sandwiches

12 Kirkland Signature Butter
    Croissants
2 16-ounce packages fresh or
    thawed mixed berries
    (e.g., strawberries, blueberries,
    raspberries)
1 tablespoon sugar
1 cup cold milk
1 package (4-serving size) instant
    cheesecake pudding
1 8-ounce tub whipped topping,
    thawed
Confectioners' sugar
Fresh strawberries, optional

1. Preheat oven to 350°F.

2. Split croissants in half horizontally with a serrated knife and keep
together. Place on a cookie sheet and bake for 8-10 minutes, or until
crust is flaky.

3. Mix berries with sugar in a medium bowl.

4. Pour milk into a medium bowl and add pudding mix. Beat with a
wire whisk for 2 minutes. Gently stir in whipped topping.

5. To assemble, spread 1/2 cup of cheesecake filling on bottom croissant
slice. Layer on 1/2 cup of berry mixture and then the croissant top.
Dust with confectioners' sugar and garnish with fresh strawberries.
Serve with a dollop of cheesecake filling on the side. Makes 12 servings.

Tip: Berry mixture and cheesecake filling can be made in advance
and refrigerated until ready to serve.

General Mills
Bakeries & Foodservice

J&J SNACK FOODS
Brownie Bugs ▼

Kids "bugging" you for homemade brownies? Using Kirkland Signature Brownie Cookies as a base, add colored frosting and candy decorations to create critters your kids will love to make and eat!

6 Kirkland Signature Brownie cookies

Licorice whips, gumdrops, mini marshmallows, chocolate chips, white chocolate chips and Kirkland Signature Doublenut cookies, for decoration

Cookie Frosting

COOKIE FROSTING
1 stick (4 ounces) butter, softened
3 cups confectioners' sugar
1 teaspoon vanilla extract
3 tablespoons milk
Food coloring

1. Place butter in a mixing bowl and beat until creamy. Gradually beat in confectioners' sugar. Mix in vanilla extract and milk until smooth.

2. Add desired food coloring to small batches of frosting. Spoon frosting into zip-top plastic bags with a tiny corner cut off the bag to allow frosting to flow out. Create a lovely ladybug, a buzzy bee or a wacky bug of your own. Let the kids go crazy! Makes 6 servings.

Ladybug: Spread red frosting over the cookie, leaving a semicircle of cookie unfrosted for the ladybug's head. Lay a licorice whip down the center of the cookie and press into the frosting. For the eyes, make 2 small dabs of frosting and apply 2 mini marshmallows. Create eye detail and the ladybug's spots using chocolate chips.

Buzzy Bee: Make stripes with yellow frosting piped from a zip-top bag. For the eyes, slice a yellow gumdrop in half and press a chocolate chip into the cut surface of each half; adhere to the cookie with a dab of frosting. Cut a Kirkland Signature Doublenut cookie in half and attach to the cookie with frosting to create wings. Add licorice whips for antennae.

MOTT'S
Apple Sauce Brownies ▲

1 cup firmly packed brown sugar
$^1/_2$ cup margarine or butter, softened
2 eggs
1 cup Mott's* Regular or Cinnamon Apple Sauce
1 teaspoon vanilla extract
1 cup all-purpose flour
$^1/_4$ cup unsweetened cocoa
1 teaspoon cinnamon
$^1/_2$ teaspoon baking powder
$^1/_2$ teaspoon baking soda
$^1/_4$ teaspoon salt
$^1/_2$ cup chopped nuts

1. Preheat oven to 350°F. Grease a 9-inch square pan.
2. In a large bowl, combine brown sugar, margarine and eggs; mix well.
3. Stir in apple sauce and vanilla; blend thoroughly. Stir in flour, cocoa, cinnamon, baking powder, baking soda and salt; mix well. Stir in nuts. Pour into prepared pan.
4. Bake for 25-35 minutes, or until a toothpick inserted in the center comes out clean. Cool on a rack; cut into squares. Makes 16 servings.

Brands may vary by region; substitute a similar product.

M&M'S
Colorful Caramel Bites ▲

1 cup plus 6 tablespoons all-purpose flour, divided
1 cup quick-cooking or old-fashioned oats, uncooked
$^3/_4$ cup firmly packed light brown sugar
$^1/_2$ teaspoon baking soda
$^1/_4$ teaspoon salt
$^3/_4$ cup butter or margarine, melted
1 $^3/_4$ cups M&M'S Milk Chocolate Candies, divided
1 $^1/_2$ cups chopped pecans, divided
1 12-ounce jar caramel ice cream topping

1. Preheat oven to 350°F.
2. Combine 1 cup flour, oats, brown sugar, baking soda and salt in a bowl. Blend in melted butter to form a crumbly mixture. Press half of the crumb mixture onto the bottom of a 9-by-9-inch baking pan; bake for 10 minutes.
3. Sprinkle with 1 cup M&M'S Candies and 1 cup pecans. Blend remaining 6 tablespoons flour with caramel topping; pour over top. Combine remaining crumb mixture, remaining $^3/_4$ cup M&M'S Candies and remaining $^1/_2$ cup pecans; sprinkle over caramel layer.
4. Bake for 20-25 minutes, or until golden brown. Makes 36 bars.

SARA LEE
Bread Pudding with
White Chocolate Sauce ▼

6 cups cubed Sara Lee* Honey Wheat Bread
2 cups peeled, cored and chopped tart apples
2 ¹/₄ cups whipping cream, divided
³/₄ cup sugar
2 eggs, beaten
¹/₃ cup each: chopped dried apricots,
     sweetened dried cranberries and coconut
1 tablespoon butter, melted
1 ¹/₂ teaspoons ground cinnamon
1 teaspoon vanilla extract
6 ounces white chocolate, chopped
Toasted coconut for garnish

1. Preheat oven to 350°F. Line 2 mini loaf pans (7 ¹/₂ by 3 ³/₄ inches) with aluminum foil; coat lightly with nonstick cooking spray.

2. In a large bowl, combine bread, apples, 1 ¹/₂ cups cream, sugar, eggs, apricots, cranberries, coconut, butter, cinnamon and vanilla. Stir until bread is moistened. Pour into the prepared pans.

3. Bake for 40-45 minutes, or until a knife inserted in the center comes out clean. Cool on a wire rack. Lift pudding out of pan, remove foil and slice.

4. To prepare sauce, microwave ³/₄ cup cream on high for 1 minute, or until it starts to simmer. Add white chocolate and whisk until smooth.

5. Serve warm sauce with the bread pudding. Garnish with toasted coconut. Makes 6 servings.

Brands may vary by region; substitute a similar product.

Desserts **I**

KIRKLAND SIGNATURE/PURATOS
Danish Pudding ▼

2 or 3 large eggs
1/4 cup sugar
2 cups whole milk
2-3 whole Kirkland Signature/Puratos Danish
   (fruited or crumb topped)
Optional:
3-4 pieces crystallized ginger, chopped, or
3 tablespoons mini chocolate chips or
3 tablespoons chopped walnuts and/or
3 tablespoons sweetened dried cranberries

1. Preheat oven to 350°F.

2. For a soft custard use 2 eggs; for a firm, sliceable Danish pudding use 3 eggs. In a medium bowl, beat eggs with a whisk; add sugar and milk.

3. Cut fresh or day-old Danish into 1/2-inch cubes; place in a greased 8-by-8-inch square pan, 8-inch glass baking dish or 6 individual custard cups. Sprinkle with ginger, chocolate chips, nuts or dried cranberries.

4. Pour custard mix over Danish cubes, pressing down with a spoon to ensure that they are evenly soaked.

5. Place pan or cups in a larger pan containing 1/2 inch of warm water. Bake 45 minutes for the pan or baking dish, or 30-35 minutes for the cups, or until the custard is set. Serve warm or cold. Makes 6-8 servings.

Serving suggestion: Spoon some berry sauce onto a dessert plate. Arrange thin slices of chilled pudding across the top and drizzle with chocolate sauce.

PURATOS

RAINIER FRUIT
Caramel Apple Bars ▲

1 ¼ cups all-purpose flour, divided
¾ cup firmly packed brown sugar, divided
½ cup (1 stick) butter or margarine
2 large eggs
1 teaspoon vanilla extract
2 Rainier Fruit* Golden Delicious apples, cored and chopped
1 cup caramel candies, each cut in quarters
½ cup chopped walnuts or pecans

1. Heat oven to 350°F. Lightly grease a 9-inch square baking pan.
2. In a medium-size bowl, combine 1 cup flour and ¼ cup brown sugar. Cut in butter until mixture resembles coarse crumbs. Transfer mixture to the pan and press down in an even layer. Bake for 10 minutes.
3. In the same mixing bowl, beat eggs. Stir in vanilla, ½ cup brown sugar and ¼ cup flour. Stir in apples, caramels and nuts. Pour over the bottom crust. Bake 30-35 minutes, or until golden. Cool slightly; cut into quarters lengthwise and crosswise. Cool completely. Makes 16 servings.

Brands may vary by region; substitute a similar product.
Courtesy of Washington Apple Commission.

EAGLE FAMILY FOODS
Magic Cookie Bars ▲

½ cup (1 stick) margarine or butter
1 ½ cups graham cracker crumbs
1 14-ounce can Eagle Brand* Sweetened Condensed Milk (NOT evaporated milk)
2 cups (12 ounces) semisweet chocolate chips
1 ⅓ cups flaked coconut
1 cup chopped walnuts

1. Preheat oven to 350°F (325°F for glass dish). Place margarine in a 9-by-13-inch pan and melt in the oven.
2. Sprinkle graham cracker crumbs over margarine; pour condensed milk evenly over crumbs. Layer remaining ingredients evenly in the order listed; press down firmly.
3. Bake for 25 minutes, or until lightly browned. Cool and cut into bars. Store loosely covered at room temperature. Makes 24-36 bars.

7-Layer Magic Cookie Bars: Substitute 1 cup butterscotch-flavored chips, peanut-butter-flavored chips or white chocolate chips for 1 cup of the semisweet chocolate chips and proceed as directed above.

Peanut Magic Cookie Bars: Substitute 1 ½ cups crushed vanilla wafers for the graham cracker crumbs, one 12-ounce package of semisweet chocolate chunks for the chocolate chips and 1 cup chopped peanuts for the walnuts.

Rainbow Magic Cookie Bars: Substitute 2 cups plain candy-coated chocolate candies for the chocolate chips.

Magnolia Sweetened Condensed Milk is an acceptable substitute.
Brands may vary by region; substitute a similar product.

SUGAR BOWL BAKERY
Petite Palmier Napoleon

3/4 cup heavy cream
3 tablespoons sugar
3 1/2 ounces (about 1/2 cup) mascarpone cheese
1 teaspoon vanilla extract
3 Sugar Bowl Bakery* Petite Palmiers
2 ounces bittersweet chocolate
Sliced strawberries
Mixed berries, optional

1. In a medium bowl, whip cream and sugar until medium peaks form. Add mascarpone and vanilla and whip until firm.
2. Toast Petite Palmiers for 1 minute, or until crispy.
3. Melt chocolate in a bowl set over a pan of simmering water.
4. Drizzle the melted chocolate on a white plate. Lay 1 palmier on the chocolate; spread with half of mascarpone cream. Add a layer of sliced strawberries. Repeat for a second layer and top with a palmier. Drizzle with melted chocolate. Garnish with strawberries and mixed berries (if desired). Makes 2 servings.

* Brands may vary by region; substitute a similar product.

COUNTRYSIDE BAKING
Black and White Rugala

1 6-ounce package semisweet chocolate chips
1 6-ounce package white chocolate chips
12 pieces Countryside* Rugala

1. Melt semisweet chocolate chips and white chocolate chips in separate bowls, according to package directions.
2. Dip each piece of rugala halfway into the melted semisweet chocolate. Set aside and let chocolate harden.
3. Dip uncoated half of the rugala into the melted white chocolate. Set aside and let harden. Makes 12 servings.
Variation: Drizzle melted semisweet chocolate and white chocolate onto the rugala with a spoon, making your own design.

* Brands may vary by region; substitute a similar product.

Countryside
Baking Co. Inc.

DANNON
Dreamy Peach Parfait ▲

2 cups Dannon* Light 'n Fit Strawberry Nonfat Yogurt

2 fresh peaches, pitted and diced, or one 15-ounce can
    cling peaches in their own juice, drained and diced

¹/₂ cup granola

1. Place ¹/₄ cup yogurt in each of four 6-ounce glasses or plastic cups.

2. Top with ¹/₄ cup diced peaches, followed by 1 tablespoon granola.

3. Repeat this layering process in each glass. Makes 4 servings.

Variation: Also try using other Dannon yogurt varieties, including Plain,
Natural Flavors Vanilla, Light 'n Fit Vanilla and Light 'n Fit Cherry Vanilla.

Brands may vary by region; substitute a similar product.

KOZY SHACK
Apple Crumble Rice Pudding ▲

¹/₂ cup butter, softened

1 cup crisp rice cereal

1 cup dark brown sugar

1 cup apple pie filling

3 cups Kozy Shack* Original Rice Pudding
    (6 individual 4-ounce containers)

6 ramekins or small ovenproof dishes

1. Preheat oven to 350°F.

2. Combine butter, cereal and brown sugar in a bowl.

3. Spoon 3 tablespoons of apple pie filling into each ramekin.
Add ¹/₂ cup (1 individual 4-ounce container) rice pudding to each
ramekin. Sprinkle each with 1 tablespoon of topping mixture.

4. Bake for 15 minutes, or until heated through. Serve warm.
Makes 6 servings.

Brands may vary by region; substitute a similar product.

Desserts ▌

KIRKLAND SIGNATURE/MULTIFOODS
Apple Pie on the Run ▼

1 Kirkland Signature fresh-baked apple pie from Costco Bakery
Waffle ice cream cones
Kirkland Signature vanilla ice cream
Caramel sundae syrup
Chopped nuts (pecans, walnuts or your choice)

1. Use an ice cream scoop for both the pie and ice cream. Place a small scoop of pie in the bottom of a waffle cone. Layer 1 small scoop of ice cream, 1 small scoop of pie, 1 scoop of ice cream, 1 scoop of pie, and finish with a nicely rounded scoop of ice cream.

2. Top with caramel syrup and sprinkle with nuts. Makes 20-24 servings.

Variation: Multifoods Apple Pie Parfait

If you have time to sit and enjoy your pie but are tired of the traditional wedge, follow instructions for Apple Pie on the Run but serve in a tulip parfait glass instead of a waffle cone.

Multifoods™

KIRKLAND SIGNATURE/MULTIFOODS
Lemon-Blueberry Trifle

1 12-ounce tub whipped dessert topping, thawed, divided
1 10-ounce jar lemon curd
3 Kirkland Signature blueberry muffins, cut in 3/4-inch chunks
1 21-ounce can wild blueberry pie filling
1 pint fresh blueberries (reserve a few for garnish)
Grated fresh lemon peel

1. Reserve 2 cups of the dessert topping. Remove lid from lemon curd and microwave the jar for about 1 minute to soften; stir. This makes it easier to spread.

2. In a 2-quart glass bowl, layer lemon curd, remaining dessert topping, muffin chunks, blueberry pie filling and fresh blueberries, in that order. Continue layering until all ingredients are used, approximately 3 layers, ending with lemon curd. Top with the reserved dessert topping.

3. Garnish with lemon peel and reserved fresh blueberries.
Makes 10-12 servings.

Variation: Use Kirkland Signature lemon poppy seed muffins.

DIAMOND FRUIT GROWERS
Pear-Strawberry Trifle

2 Diamond Fruit Growers* winter pears, peeled, cored and thinly sliced
2 tablespoons lemon juice
2 cups coarsely chopped strawberries
2 tablespoons almond-flavored liqueur, or 1/2 teaspoon almond extract
2 tablespoons orange juice
2 tablespoons honey
1/2 9-inch angel food cake, cut in 1-inch cubes
3 cups vanilla- or lemon-flavored yogurt
1 cup diced fresh or drained canned pineapple
Pear slices and mint sprigs for garnish

1. Toss pears in lemon juice and strawberries in liqueur. Combine orange juice and honey; mix well.

2. In a deep 2- to 2 1/2-quart glass bowl, layer ingredients in the following order: 1/3 of cake sprinkled with 1 tablespoon orange juice mixture, 1 cup yogurt, 1 cup pears, 1 cup strawberries and 1/2 cup pineapple; repeat.

3. Top with remaining cake, sprinkle with remaining orange juice mixture, and spread 1 cup yogurt over top. Cover with plastic wrap and refrigerate 1-4 hours. Garnish with pear slices and mint just before serving.
Makes 6 servings.

Brands may vary by region; substitute a similar product.

Desserts I

CAFFE D'VITA
Mocha Cappuccino Crème Brûlée ▲

6 egg yolks
$1/4$ cup plus 6 tablespoons sugar
$1/2$ cup Caffe D'Vita* Cappuccino mix
$3/4$ cup hot water
$1 1/2$ cups whipping cream
$1/2$ cup half-and-half
1 teaspoon vanilla extract

1. Preheat oven to 325°F.

2. Blend egg yolks and $1/4$ cup sugar in a bowl. Mix Caffe D'Vita with the hot water; stir into the egg yolks. Add cream, half-and-half and vanilla extract, stirring until thoroughly combined.

3. Pour mixture into six $1/2$-cup ramekins and place in a baking pan. Add enough boiling water to the pan to reach halfway up the sides of the ramekins. Bake for 40 minutes, or until custard is set. Remove the custards from the pan. Let cool, then refrigerate until well chilled.

4. When ready to serve, preheat broiler. Sprinkle the top of each custard with 1 tablespoon sugar. Place ramekins under a very hot broiler until the sugar caramelizes. Serve immediately. Makes 6 servings.

* Brands may vary by region; substitute a similar product.

LINDOR TRUFFLES
Chocolate Mousse ▲

9 Dark Lindor Truffles
5 Milk Lindor Truffles
3 large eggs, separated
1 tablespoon granulated sugar
$1 1/4$ cups whipping cream
2 tablespoons
   confectioners' sugar
1 teaspoon vanilla extract

GARNISH
Lindor Truffles
Whipped cream

1. Unwrap dark and milk truffles and melt in a double boiler over medium heat. Remove from heat.

2. Whisk egg yolks in a bowl until foamy. Add a small amount of the melted chocolate to the eggs and whisk in. Whisk in remaining chocolate.

3. In a bowl, beat egg whites and granulated sugar until stiff peaks form. Fold into the chocolate/egg mixture.

4. Whip cream, confectioners' sugar and vanilla until fluffy. Fold into the chocolate mixture.

5. Pour mousse into serving dishes and chill for 8 hours or overnight. Garnish each serving with a truffle and whipped cream, if desired. Makes 6-8 servings.

Tip: For White Chocolate Mousse, replace Milk and Dark Lindor Truffles with 14 White Lindor Truffles.

TRINITY FRUIT
Fresh Fruit Compote ▲

$^1/_2$ pound each peaches, plums and nectarines, halved and pitted
1 cup sugar
Juice of 1 lemon
$^1/_4$ cup apple juice
1 teaspoon vanilla extract
3 cinnamon sticks
2 cloves
$^1/_2$ pound Asian pears, quartered or sliced, depending on size
$^1/_4$ pound cherries, halved and pitted
$^1/_2$ cup amaretto, optional
Vanilla ice cream
Whipped cream

1. Blanch peaches, plums and nectarines in hot water to cover; remove peel.
2. Place sugar, lemon juice and apple juice in a large saucepan and bring to a boil; simmer for 2 minutes. Add vanilla, cinnamon and cloves. Adjust heat to just below boiling and add peaches, plums, nectarines, Asian pears and cherries. Simmer for 5-8 minutes, or until soft.
3. Remove from heat; pour amaretto over fruit and let cool. Remove fruit and cook liquid to reduce to a syrupy consistency; let cool.
4. Return fruit to syrup, gently stirring. Serve warm or cold over ice cream and finish with a dollop of whipped cream. Makes 6 servings.
Recipe provided by Erna's Elderberry House.

PRIMAVERA
Cherries Jubilee ▲

1 16-ounce can Bing cherries
1 teaspoon arrowroot
1 teaspoon freshly squeezed lemon juice
1 cup sugar, plus more for flaming
40 fresh pitted California Bing cherries
$^1/_4$ cup kirsch (cherry brandy)
3 tablespoons Cognac
Vanilla ice cream

1. Pour juice from the can of cherries into a large, shallow saucepan. In a small bowl, stir together arrowroot and lemon juice; add to the saucepan and mix well. Stir in 1 cup sugar; cook over high heat, stirring constantly, until it is the consistency of a thick syrup. Lower heat and simmer for 10 minutes.
2. Add fresh cherries to the syrup and simmer for 5 minutes. Heat the kirsch and Cognac; add to the sauce. Remove the pan from the heat.
3. Sprinkle the surface with sugar (don't stir in). Stand back and ignite. Serve hot over your favorite vanilla ice cream. Makes 6-8 servings.

JELLY BELLY
Meringue Nests with Jelly Beans ▼

6 egg whites
Pinch of salt
1 ¹/₂ teaspoons cream of tartar
¹/₂ teaspoon almond extract
1 ¹/₂ cups sugar
4 ounces assorted Jelly Belly jelly beans (Cotton Candy, Berry Blue, Lemon Drop, Island Punch and Lemon Lime flavors)
Candies or sherbet to fill nests

1. Preheat oven to 170°F.

2. Line a baking sheet with parchment paper. Using a round cookie cutter or a small can, trace ten 3¹/₂- to 4-inch circles. Set aside.

3. In the clean, dry bowl of an electric mixer, beat egg whites, salt and cream of tartar until soft peaks form. With the beater running, add almond extract and then gradually add sugar; beat until stiff and glossy.

4. Spoon about ³/₄ cup meringue onto the parchment-lined baking sheet, using the tracing lines as a guide for size. With a large spoon, make an indentation in each meringue mound to form a nest.

5. Gently press jelly beans into sides of meringues. Bake for 2 ¹/₂ hours, or until hard.

6. Fill meringues with jelly beans or other assorted candies. For an elegant dessert, fill meringue nests with small scoops of pastel sherbets. Serve immediately. Makes 10 nests.

Tip: Nests can be made 2 days ahead and stored in an airtight container.

SunWest
Summer Fruit Granita

1 pound fresh ripe SunWest* California peaches, plums or nectarines
1/2 cup sugar
1/2 cup fresh or frozen raspberries (only if using nectarines)
1/4 cup fresh orange juice
2 tablespoons fresh lemon juice

1. Cut fruit into a large saucepan, discarding the pits. Add sugar and 1 cup water; bring to a boil. Reduce heat, cover and let simmer for 10 minutes, or until fruit is tender. Let fruit cool; add raspberries if using nectarines.
2. Pour fruit into a blender and purée. Strain through a sieve; discard any pulp. Stir in orange and lemon juice; taste for sweetness, adding sugar as needed.
3. Pour into a 9-inch square nonreactive metal or glass pan. Cover and freeze until ice crystals form around the edges, about 30 minutes. With a fork, stir the ice crystals toward the center. Repeat process once or twice before it is completely frozen to create a granular texture.
4. Break up the frozen mixture with a fork or chop with a chef's knife. Serve in stemmed glasses. Makes 4 servings.

Brands may vary by region; substitute a similar product.

Martinelli's
Sparkling Cider à la Mode

8 ounces Martinelli's* Sparkling Cider (well chilled)
1 scoop vanilla ice cream
Cinnamon
Whipped cream
Nutmeg
Apple wedge

1. Put sparkling cider and ice cream in a blender and mix thoroughly.
2. Add cinnamon to taste. Pour into a glass and garnish with whipped cream, a sprinkle of nutmeg and an apple wedge. Makes 1 superb after-dinner drink.

Brands may vary by region; substitute a similar product.

Martinelli's
SINCE 1868
GOLD MEDAL®

Beverages

HOLTZINGER FRUIT
Cherry-Berry Smoothie ◀

**3 cups Holtzinger Fruit* fresh pitted
dark sweet cherries**
3 cups frozen whole strawberries (unsweetened)
3 cups cran-cherry juice

1. In a blender, purée half the fresh pitted dark sweet cherries,
half the frozen strawberries and half the cran-cherry juice,
stirring as needed, until smooth.

2. Pour into 2 serving glasses. Repeat with the remaining
ingredients for 2 more servings. Makes four 12-ounce servings.

Variation: When out of season, replace fresh cherries with two
15-ounce cans pitted dark sweet cherries, well drained, and 6 ice cubes.

* Brands may vary by region; substitute a similar product.

SPLENDA
Strawberry Orange Smash ▲

2 1/2 cups unsweetened frozen strawberries
1/2 cup Splenda No Calorie Sweetener, Granular
1 cup calcium-fortified orange juice
3/4 cup plain fat-free yogurt
1/2 teaspoon vanilla extract
1/4 cup crushed ice

Process all ingredients in a blender until smooth, stopping
to scrape down sides. Serve immediately. Makes 4 servings.

LIPTON
Beat-the-Heat Tea Shake

6 Lipton "Brisk" Cup-Size Tea Bags
1 quart boiling water
1 pint any flavor sherbet or ice cream
Strawberries for garnish

1. Place tea bags in a teapot; pour boiling water over the tea bags. Cover and brew for 3-5 minutes. Remove tea bags; chill.
2. In a 5-cup blender, combine 2 1/2 cups tea with sherbet or ice cream; process at high speed until blended. Garnish, if desired, with whole strawberries. Makes 4 servings.

OREGON CHAI
Banana Smoothie

4 ounces Oregon Chai* Original Chai concentrate
4 ounces yogurt, whole milk or dairy base
1 medium banana (4 ounces), peeled
2 ounces crushed ice (2 cubes)

Place chai concentrate, yogurt, banana and ice in a blender. Purée and serve immediately. Makes 1 serving.

Tip: Use this mixture as a base and toss in raspberries, blackberries, pears, kiwis or mangoes.

* Brands may vary by region; substitute a similar product.

APPLE & EVE
Ruby Fruit Smoothie ▲

2 cups frozen sliced peaches
6 ounces canned mandarin oranges, drained
8 ounces Apple & Eve* Ruby Red Grapefruit Juice Cocktail
4 ounces pineapple juice
1 large scoop frozen vanilla yogurt

All ingredients should be chilled before use. Combine all ingredients in a blender. Cover and blend until smooth. Pour into tall glasses and garnish with sliced peaches. Makes 4-6 servings.

Tip: For a thicker smoothie, add more frozen peaches.

Brands may vary by region; substitute a similar product.

KIRKLAND SIGNATURE
Tangy Berry Smoothie ▲

2 cups Kirkland Signature cranberry juice
1 cup vanilla yogurt
1 pint fresh strawberries, hulled, or 16 ounces frozen strawberries
1 banana

Combine all ingredients in a blender and purée. Makes 5-6 servings.
Variation: Pour into ice pop molds and enjoy as a healthy frozen treat.

CLIFFSTAR CORPORATION

SUGAR FOODS
Lemonade with Ginger ▲

4 1/2 cups water, divided
1/4 cup sugar
4 thin slices fresh ginger
1/4 cup plus 2 tablespoons fresh lemon juice
1 packet Sweet'N Low* granulated sugar substitute
Lime slices

1. In a medium saucepan over medium-high heat, bring 3 1/2 cups water, sugar and ginger to a boil. Remove from heat and cool for 10 minutes.
2. Stir in lemon juice, Sweet'N Low and enough water to equal 4 cups. Refrigerate until well chilled.
3. Remove ginger and serve over ice; garnish with lime slices.
Makes 4 servings.

Brands may vary by region; substitute a similar product.

MARTINELLI'S
Sparkler ▲

8 ounces Martinelli's* Sparkling Cider (well chilled)
2 splashes of grenadine
1 splash of Rose's Lime Juice
Maraschino cherry, for garnish
Lemon wedge, for garnish

Fill a tall highball glass with ice. Add sparkling cider, grenadine and lime juice. Garnish with a maraschino cherry and a lemon wedge.
Makes 1 great cocktail without the alcohol.

Brands may vary by region; substitute a similar product.

DOMEX
Cherry-Lemon Cooler ▲

3 cups water
1 cup sugar
1 cup Northwest fresh sweet cherries, halved and pitted
Crushed ice
1 cup chilled fresh lemon juice
1 1-liter bottle club soda or seltzer
Northwest fresh sweet cherries with stems
4 long stems of fresh mint

1. Combine water and sugar in a small saucepan; add cherries. Bring to a boil, reduce heat and simmer for 5 minutes. Remove from heat and let cool to room temperature. Strain syrup into a container with a tight-fitting lid; discard cherries. Refrigerate syrup until cold.
2. Fill a tall 12- to 16-ounce glass with ice. Pour $1/4$ cup lemon juice and $1/3$ cup syrup over ice; top with club soda. Garnish with cherries and mint. Makes 4 servings.

Tip: Leftover syrup can be stored, refrigerated, for up to 1 week.

Recipe courtesy of Northwest Cherry Growers.

TREE TOP
Hot Apple Cinnamon Fluffs ▲

4 cups Tree Top* Apple Juice or Apple Cider
1 cup marshmallow creme or fluff
1 teaspoon vanilla extract
1 teaspoon ground cinnamon
$1/2$ teaspoon ground nutmeg

1. Heat apple juice and pour into 4 mugs.
2. Place marshmallow creme in a bowl and stir in vanilla, cinnamon and nutmeg.
3. Spoon the marshmallow mixture on top of the warm juice and serve. Yum! Makes 4 servings.

* Brands may vary by region; substitute a similar product.

SAN FRANCISCO BAY
Iced Coffee ▲

Ingredients: Use fresh cold or bottled water and San Francisco Bay* Gourmet Coffee—top quality, custom roasted and absolutely fresh.

Grinding: Grind coffee beans just before using. Espresso should be almost powdery, drip filter should look about like sand, and the grind for slower methods should be a little coarser.

Method: You will be diluting the coffee over ice, so you should make it twice as strong as usual. You can do this by using either half the amount of water you usually use or twice the amount of coffee. After brewing, cool the coffee for at least 10 minutes. For something different, try adding 1/4 teaspoon vanilla extract or 2 ounces chocolate syrup per 6-cup pot. Once the coffee is cool, pour it directly over ice.

Tips: Add milk or cream if desired, and sweetener to taste. Try whipping it in a blender for a delicious coffee frappe.

Brands may vary by region; substitute a similar product.

KIRKLAND SIGNATURE
Iced Café Mocha ▲

4 cups chilled Kirkland Signature coffee
1 1/2 cups milk
1/4 cup instant chocolate milk powder
1 1/2 cups plus 1/4 cup whipping cream
4 scoops vanilla ice cream
Nutmeg
Cinnamon

1. Pour chilled coffee, milk and instant chocolate milk powder into a blender; mix together. Add 1 1/2 cups whipping cream and ice cream; blend well.

2. Pour the remaining 1/4 cup cream into a small bowl and beat until stiff peaks form.

3. Pour the coffee drink into tall glasses. Garnish with whipped cream, nutmeg and cinnamon to taste. Makes 8 servings.

Coffee & Tea

ENJOY THE PERFECT CUP OF COFFEE AT HOME.

How you store, grind and brew your coffee is just as important as which coffee you choose. To ensure a consistent, delicious cup, Starbucks offers some coffee brewing wisdom.

1. **Proper storage will help maintain the freshness and flavor of your coffee.**

   Starbucks FlavorLock bag protects the coffee from air, light and moisture. Once the bag is opened, coffee should be used within seven days. Store beans in an airtight container in a cool, dry place.

2. **Use fresh, cold water.**

   Water is 98% of every cup; for best results, consider using filtered water or bottled water.

3. **We recommend using 2 tbsp (10 g) of ground coffee for each 6 fl oz (180 mL) of water.**

   Keep these proportions consistent, regardless of the quantity you make. To moderate your coffee's strength, simply add hot water after brewing.

4. **Use the correct grind for your coffeemaker.**

   Too fine a grind will cause bitter tasting coffee or clog your brewer. Too coarse a grind will cause watery coffee. For drip brewers, the appropriate grind should allow the coffee to finish dripping in several minutes. Coffee presses require a coarse grind; espresso machines require a very fine grind.

5. **Boiling causes bitterness, so never boil coffee.**

   It should be brewed between 195° F and 205° F (90° C and 96° C) to extract the coffee's full range of flavors.

6. **Coffee can be kept warm over a burner for only about 20 minutes before the flavor becomes unpleasant.**

   A thermal carafe will keep coffee hot and delicious for much longer periods of time.

7. **Do not reheat coffee.**

   Make it fresh each time you serve it, and make only as much as you plan to drink. Coffee holds its flavor best at 186° F (86° C).

WITH THE RIGHT COFFEE AND THE PROPER TECHNIQUES, YOU'RE ON YOUR WAY TO BREWING THE PERFECT CUP.

Index I

Index I

Index I

Vendor Listing I

Notes **I**

Notes